BRITISH CASTLES

CONWY CASTLE 1913 65753P

BRITISH CASTLES

WITH PHOTOGRAPHS FROM THE FRANCIS FRITH COLLECTION

Compiled and edited by Julia Skinner and Eliza Sackett

Bounty
Books

First published in the United Kingdom in 2006 by The Francis Frith Collection for Bounty Books
a division of Octopus Publishing Group,
2-4 Heron Quays, London E14 4JP, England

Hardback edition ISBN 10: 0-7537-1443-4
ISBN 13: 978-0-7537-1443-0

British Library Cataloguing in Publication Data

British Castles
Compiled and edited by Julia Skinner and Eliza Sackett

The Francis Frith Collection
Frith's Barn, Teffont,
Salisbury, Wiltshire SP3 5QP
Tel: +44 (0) 1722 716 376
Email: info@francisfrith.co.uk
www.francisfrith.com

Designed and assembled by David Davies

Printed in Singapore by Imago

Front Cover: Richmond, The Castle and the Bridge 1893 32275T

The colour-tinting in this book is for illustrative purposes only, and is not intended to be historically accurate.

Every attempt has been made to contact copyright holders of illustrative material.
We will be happy to give full acknowledgement in future editions for any items not credited.
Any information should be directed to The Francis Frith Collection.

AS WITH ANY HISTORICAL DATABASE, THE FRANCIS FRITH ARCHIVE IS CONSTANTLY BEING CORRECTED AND IMPROVED,
AND THE PUBLISHERS WOULD WELCOME INFORMATION ON OMISSIONS OR INACCURACIES

CONTENTS

Introduction   6

The West Country   10

London & The South   24

The Midlands & East Anglia   45

The North   58

Wales   88

Scotland   127

Index   155

Voucher for Free Mounted Print   159

BRITISH CASTLES - INTRODUCTION

THE NORMAN CONQUEST

The Normans introduced castles to Britain (a very few castles were built before the Norman Conquest, but these were built by Norman lords who had settled here); had it not been for the Norman invasion, we would not have the rich heritage of castles that we do today.

1066 is sometimes referred to as 'The Year of Three Kings' - Edward the Confessor, Harold II and William I all wore the crown of England in this year. William the Conqueror's claim to the throne was very slight indeed. He was a distant cousin of the English King Edward, nicknamed 'the Confessor' for his piety, who had been brought up in Normandy. William himself considered that his right to the English throne stemmed from a promise made to him by the childless King Edward in 1051, nominating him as his heir, although under Anglo-Saxon law this was not merely a matter for the king to decide; the powerful Anglo-Saxon nobleman Harold Godwinson of Wessex was actually the choice of the Witan, the council of wise men and other notables who advised the King of England. William set great store by this promise of King Edward, and his belief in his right to the throne was strengthened when Harold Godwinson swore on holy relics to support William's claim after visiting, or being shipwrecked on, Normandy in 1064. Some versions of the oath say that Harold was tricked into it, with the sacred relics being hidden under the table; others that the oath was made under duress, with Harold being held prisoner until he had agreed to it. Whatever the truth, Harold himself obviously did not consider the oath to be

AN ARTIST'S IMPRESSION OF A NORMAN SHIP, FROM THE BAYEUX TAPESTRY F6019

binding; when King Edward died, the Witan appointed Harold to be king, and he agreed.

The issue became even more complicated with the arrival on the scene of a third claimant to the throne, King Harald Hardrada of Norway. His claim was even more tenuous, but he arrived in northern England with an invasion force in September 1066, assisted by Tostig Godwinson, Harold's brother. Harold and his Anglo-Saxon forces made a swift forced march north, and defeated the Norwegian forces conclusively at the battle of Stamford Bridge, near York. Both Harald Hardrada and Tostig were killed, and the remains of the Norwegian army fled to their ships – only 24 of the original fleet of 240 ships returned home. But Harold's enjoyment of his victory was short-lived, as news was brought to him that William of Normandy had just landed on the Sussex coast.

William had been making his preparations to claim the throne for many months, and all that had delayed him was the need to wait for a favourable wind – now the wind had changed, at the worst possible time for Harold. The Norman invasion force comprised 600 transport ships, carrying about 7,000 men and around 3,000 cavalry horses across the Channel. He landed near Pevensey on 28 September.

Harold and his exhausted, battle-weary forces marched down the 250 miles from Yorkshire in nine days, and met the Norman army at what history now calls the battle of Hastings on 14 October 1066. Both sides fought bitterly, and three of William's horses were killed under him. A chronicler described the conflict as 'one side attacking with all mobility, the other withstanding as though rooted to the soil'. After a long struggle, King Harold and two of his brothers were killed; the defeated remnants of the Anglo-Saxon forces fled, and King William had won the day.

CASTLE BUILDING AND CASTLES IN BRITISH HISTORY

The word 'castle' conjures up different things to different people: knights in armour, damsels in distress, robber barons, Robin Hood and the Sheriff of Nottingham and so on. But the main purpose of a castle was as a fortified residence from which a lord could exert control over the surrounding area.

The castle as a means of exercising political, social and military control over an area was developed in Normandy in the years before the Norman Conquest of

England. There were a handful of castles in England before the Norman Conquest, built by Norman lords who had settled in the country at the invitation of the pro-Norman Edward the Confessor, such as those at Hereford, Ewyas Harold and Richard's Castle in Herefordshire, but it was under William the Conqueror that the landscape of Britain began to be dominated by these forceful symbols of strength and power.

Following the Norman invasion, a considerable number of motte-and-bailey castles with wooden towers and palisades were thrown up in order to assert immediate control over the newly conquered population. Many of these would be abandoned as feudal authority was asserted, but others would become far more permanent, their wooden structures eventually replaced by new buildings of stone. Within a short space of time the knight and the castle would become the embodiment of warfare in the feudal period. The ethos of the time was such that besieging a castle, and the etiquette associated with it, would be just as important as fighting a pitched battle, and the age of chivalry was born.

The anarchy of King Stephen's reign (1135-54) meant that lords and landowners needed defendable strongholds, and hundreds of castles were built during this period. By the late 12th century the updating of earlier castles and the building of new stone castles dominated the royal policies of Henry II, Richard I and King John. Sums spent varied from one castle to another: the keep at Dover cost Henry II the sum of £4,000, though he probably spent around £7,000 on the castle in total, and the Tower of London cost £2,400. By around 1200 any great lord obtaining a licence to crenellate not only had the construction costs to find (and these could be considerable), but would have to commit £100-150 a year to cover running costs. Castle design was constantly developing to take into account new weaponry and siege warfare techniques – most castles that had an adequate food and water supply were practically impregnable by direct assault, and when attacked both sides resigned themselves to a lengthy sit-and-wait period until the matter was either resolved by starvation or the arrival of a relieving force.

The reign of Edward I (1272-1307) marked the climax of royal castle building. Edward enforced the conquest of Wales by building vast and strong fortresses, some of the finest in the country. Later, Edward III (1327-1377) embarked on more building – his fear of invasion from France led him to strengthen and build castles, and many private houses were granted licences to crenellate.

In the later medieval period castles were both the homes of the great nobles who held them, and also the barracks of large numbers of their armed retainers. They represented threatening centres of power against the monarch, and most kings of the Middle Ages found themselves in constant power struggles with their barons. After what later became known as the Wars of the Roses (which were in effect a series of pitched battles between the private armies of rival claimants to the throne), these large private armies were correctly perceived as a threat by Henry VII. He passed laws against 'livery' (flaunting your power by giving your adherents badges and emblems) and 'maintenance' (keeping too many male 'servants', a euphemism for soldiers). These laws were used very shrewdly in levying fines upon those that he perceived as dangerously powerful.

During the Civil War many castles were the scene of sieges or bitter battles, often changing hands several times during the course of the war. With their men away fighting for the king or for Parliament, the defence of the castles was often undertaken by the womenfolk – an example is the defence of Corfe in Dorset by Lady Bankes. However, from the 16th century the nobility of England began building non-fortified houses, and the age of the castle in its true sense was coming to an end. Many castles were extensively refurbished, or even demolished and rebuilt, to create elegant, comfortable and impressive residences, often in a Gothic or Jacobean style. There was also a spate of new 'castle' building; although the new structures were often adorned with battlements and towers, they were in fact residences with no military value: the country house had taken over the castle's role as the main residence of the aristocracy and ruling class.

CASTLES IN WALES

William the Conqueror took little active role in the Norman expansion into Wales, content to leave it to men like William FitzOsbern. Norman inroads into Wales were slow, as the full weight of the Norman war machine could not be fully committed until the pacification of England was complete. The reign of Henry I saw Norman domination spread over much of Wales; the Gower peninsula and Pembrokeshire became so populated with colonists that the Welsh language all but disappeared from the area. Henry's death in 1135 plunged England into civil war and anarchy. The Welsh rose in rebellion under Owain Glyndwr, driving the Normans from much of North Wales. This was the beginning of a period that would see Wales produce several able and determined leaders, including Rhys ap Gruffydd, whose stronghold was at Dynevor Castle. In 1165 Welsh leaders put their differences to one side and combined their forces to defeat Henry II's Anglo-French army. The alliance did not last: Rhys and Owain Gwynedd turned on Owain Cyfeiliog, and Henry was soon back. Henry agreed to recognise Owain Gwynedd's lands in the north and Rhys's in the south.

Llywelyn ap Iorwerth (Llywelyn the Great) became ruler of Gwynedd in 1201. By 1211 his power and influence was such that his own father-in-law, King John, launched an invasion of Wales which was supported by a number of Welsh lords, forcing Llywelyn to come to terms. In 1215 Llywelyn actively sided with the barons against King John, and cemented his position by the marriages of his daughters into powerful families. The Baron's War weakened John's ability to hold Llywelyn in check, and for a few years Wales experienced a period of unity under an able leader. However, Llywelyn's death in 1240 created a power vacuum; his successor was his grandson, Llywelyn ap Gruffydd, who would be known to history as the first and only native Prince of Wales. Llywelyn's title was recognised by Henry III, and in return Llywelyn acknowledged Henry as his overlord. However, the balance of power changed drastically when Edward I succeeded his father as king. Llywelyn antagonised Edward by not attending his coronation, and then by attacking English border areas. This failure to attend the coronation was not just a discourtesy – it meant that Llywelyn had failed to pay homage to Edward as his feudal lord. It was partly an attempt to enforce his legal rights over Llywelyn that caused Edward to invade Wales.

In the summer of 1277, the able and ruthless Edward was ready to move against Llywelyn. Edward was determined not only to dispose of Llywelyn but also to stamp his authority upon the Welsh for ever, firstly by force of arms and secondly by an impressive programme of castle-building. His first aim succeeded when the head of Llywelyn was brought to him, to be displayed on a stake outside the Tower of London; and his second when he established a chain of castles, many of which still loom over many Welsh towns.

Edward I (1272-1307) spent a fortune on building six major castles and strengthening others during his wars against the Welsh. At the lower end of his expenses, £318 was spent on upgrading the defences at Criccieth. Harlech, however, took six years and £8,000 to build, and Flint a little over nine years and £7,000. Beaumaris cost £14,500 and the castle and town walls of Caernarvon together cost £19,900, an enormous sum in those days. With several castles under construction at once, Edward recruited workers from throughout England. In 1277 almost 3,000 men assembled at Chester, where they were allocated to works at Flint, Rhuddlan and elsewhere. In addition to his own enthusiastic building programme, Edward actively encouraged his loyal barons such as Payn de Chaworth to rebuild their own fortresses, often through subsidies from the Crown.

The Edwardian castles include some of the finest castles ever built in Britain, and they form a comprehensive defensive system, a huge and impressive undertaking. These castles characteristically replace the keep by a strong curtain wall with flanking towers; within the curtain there are further concentric lines of defence, and the curtain is guarded by a strong gatehouse.

As we have seen, Edward I's grandson Edward III (1327-1377), fearing invasion from France, strengthened and built castles in Wales, and also in England.

CASTLES IN SCOTLAND

Castle building came to mainland Scotland not as a result of conquest and occupation, but as a result of the deliberate policies of kings like Malcolm III (1058-1093) and David I (1124-1153), who encouraged the immigration of Anglo-Norman lords by offering land grants. Both Malcolm and David were influenced by what they had seen during their stays in England. Following his father's death, Malcolm had spent a number of years as an exile at the great Norman court of Edward the Confessor. The Norman influence on David was even stronger; having been brought up and educated at the English court, he was keen to import Norman society and the Norman-style government and feudal tenure into Scotland. When he returned to Scotland, among the many friends he brought with him were Bernard de Balleul, Robert de Brus and Walter FitzAlan.

Under David, the Anglo-Norman lords built motte-and-bailey castles with timber towers as they had in England, and within 50 years the Norman lords were holding lands as far north as the Don, the Spey and Moray. Native landowners still held their lands, but now they were tenants, bound by feudal obligations to render services to their overlords. Many of these castles were later rebuilt as stone fortresses. However, what is interesting is that these lords did not rebuild their fortresses with great stone keeps as they did south of the border; in fact, the most northern castle with a classic Norman keep is at Norham on the Tweed.

William the Lion, who reigned from 1165 to 1214, built castles at Ayr, Lanark and Dumfries in order to keep the Lords of Galloway in check, and he built Dunskaith on the Cromarty Firth and Redcastle on the Beauly Firth during his attempt to extend his rule. In the areas of Scotland under Norse rule there were a handful of castles in existence during the 12th century, but castle building did not assume any importance until the reign of Haakon IV. The 'Orkneyinga Saga' recalls the building of a small stone castle on the island of Wyre in the Orkneys by Kolbein Hruga around 1143-48; today this castle is better known as Cubbie Row, a corruption of Kolbein's name. The small tower has walls 5ft thick, and is protected by ramparts; there was no entrance to the ground floor from the outside. Other Norse castles in the Orkneys are Damsay and Cairston. Dunvaig Castle on Oslay might also be of Norse origin.

Tower-houses exist throughout Scotland, but are particularly common in the old province of Mar, between the Don and Dee valleys. The earliest appear to have been constructed in the later 13th to mid 14th centuries. Usually standing four or five storeys high, they are in effect a rethink of the medieval hall house: instead of being a series of rooms extended horizontally, here they are stacked vertically for defence. Internal arrangements varied – it often depended on how much the owner was prepared to spend – but they were strong enough to withstand most forms of attack apart from sieges. The walls of the tower were usually thickest at ground floor level, both to support the weight of the structure and for defence. The ground floor was usually vaulted for protection against fire, and in some towers the only access to this level was by an internal staircase or ladder. The main entrance was a door on the first floor reached by a ladder, which could be taken inside when danger threatened. Usually this floor contained the hall and the private chamber of the owner. As fire was often used by raiders, those owners who could afford it had their towers roofed with slate or stone. On the upper floors the tower-houses burst into a riot of corbelled-out towers and gables to increase the amount of accommodation.

The style of the tower-houses of Mar influenced later castle architects, eventually leading to the Scottish Baronial style that became so popular in the 18th and 19th centuries, when all things Scottish became fashionable, especially after the success of Sir Walter Scott's novels. The best-known example of a Baronial-style castle is Queen Victoria's beloved Balmoral, extended and designed (with professional help) by Prince Albert, which is still a summer holiday residence of the royal family.

GLOSSARY

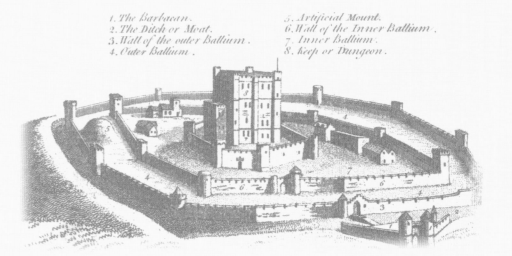

1. The Barbican.
2. The Ditch or Moat.
3. Wall of the outer Ballium.
4. Outer Ballium.
5. Artificial Mount.
6. Wall of the Inner Ballium.
7. Inner Ballium.
8. Keep or Dungeon.

Bailey: a defended courtyard or wall of a castle.

Ballium: alternative term for bailey.

Barbican: a gated outer work, usually separated by a drawbridge from the main gate of the castle.

Bastion: a projection from the main walls that allowed defenders to fire along the flanks of the fortification.

Casemate: gallery with loopholes from which the castle defenders could fire.

Castellan: the resident owner of a castle.

Constable: the governor or warden of a castle in the owner's absence – an important and responsible post.

Crenellation: the battlementing of walls. A licence to crenellate (royal consent) was required for a fortified building.

Curtain: a wall enclosing a bailey, ward or courtyard.

Donjon: keep.

Drum towers: flanking towers, circular in section.

Glacis: defensive slope.

Keep: the great tower and strong-point of a castle, also known as a donjon.

Machicolation: openings in the floor of a projecting parapet that allowed the defenders to drop missiles upon the heads of the attackers.

Motte: the mound upon which a castle was built; usually artificial.

Motte-and-bailey: early type of castle – a mound with a surrounding ditch topped by a tower with a further area defended by a ditch and palisade.

Murder holes: openings in ceilings through which attackers could be shot at.

Portcullis: a heavy grille made of wood and/or iron, protecting an entrance. It was raised or lowered by winches in the gatehouse.

Ringwork: a circular or oval-shaped defensive bank and ditch.

Shell-keep: stone building completely surrounding the summit of a motte.

Tower-house: a fortress residence, almost as strong as a castle, common in Scotland and northern England.

Ward: guarded or protected area, a courtyard or bailey.

TINTAGEL CASTLE

The castle of Tintagel possibly dates from c1145; there is a theory that the first castle here was built by Reginald, Earl of Cornwall, a bastard son of Henry I.

When the Normans reached the far west, they were told that Cornwall's ancient kings had built their stronghold on this dramatic headland. Thus it made good sense in terms of propaganda for the Normans to build here (although it made little strategic sense). Earl Richard of Cornwall, the younger brother of Henry III, erected his castle here in the 1230s. The castle was modified over the years, and the ruins we see today date from the 13th to the 15th century.

Perched on rocky cliffs five miles north-west of Camelford, Tintagel probably owes its survival to its association with the Arthurian legends. This atmospheric site on the north coast of Cornwall overlooking the sea was recorded by Geoffrey of Monmouth in the 1100s as being the birthplace of King Arthur. Geoffrey's description of the area is so accurate that it is believed that he visited the site himself: 'The castle is built high above the sea, which surrounds it on all sides, and there is no other way in except that offered by a narrow isthmus of rock'. The name 'Tintagel' derives from the Old Cornish 'din' or 'tin' (fortress) and 'tagel' (constriction or narrows).

TINTAGEL AND KING ARTHUR

There have been several archaeological excavations here, which have uncovered the remains of dozens of huts from the 5th century, the supposed Arthurian period. It appears that the area was an important centre of trade, with Cornish tin being exchanged for oil, wine, and other luxury goods from the Mediterranean; the prosperity of the area can be judged from the fact that more sherds of imported pottery have been found at Tintagel that at all the other sites of similar period in Britain and Ireland combined. During an excavation in 1998 a piece of rock was uncovered bearing a Runic inscription dating from the 500s, which includes the name 'Artognov', or 'Arthnou'. This caused great excitement in the media and was promptly dubbed 'the Arthur Stone', and was hailed as proof of the Arthurian connection with Tintagel. However, Dr Geoffrey Wainwright, chief archaeologist with English Heritage, said: 'Despite the obvious temptation to link the Arthnou stone to either the historical or the legendary figure of Arthur, it must be stressed there is no evidence to make this connection. Nevertheless it proves for the first time that the name existed at that time and that the stone belonged to a person of status.'

Left: TINTAGEL CASTLE 1894   33595A

Above: TINTAGEL CASTLE 1895   36987

Left: TINTAGEL CASTLE 1895   36989

ST MAWES CASTLE

Right: ST MAWES CASTLE 1890 24234

Below: ST MAWES CASTLE 1938 88813

The castle at St Mawes was built by order of Henry VIII in 1542 to protect the harbour. Fear of foreign invasion caused him to construct a series of coastal forts designed for artillery – two others near by are at Pendennis and St Anthony. St Mawes has a central tower and three smaller lobes, so that from the air it resembles a clover leaf. The circular keep contains four floors; the approach from the landward side is by way of a drawbridge. The castle is sited on lower ground 'the better to annoy shipping'.

HENRY VIII'S COAST DEFENCE CASTLES

In order for Henry VIII to divorce his first wife, Katherine of Aragon, to marry Anne Boleyn, the king had to break with the Church of Rome and set himself up as the head of the Church in England. By 1538, Pope Paul III was preaching for a crusade against England, and hoped that France and Spain would join forces in an invasion that would see the country returned to Papal authority. A direct result of this threat was a strengthening of the Royal Navy and the construction of a series of coast defence barriers to protect potential anchorages. There were five castles protecting the Thames between Tilbury and Gravesend; the Sandown, Deal and Walmer chain covering the Downs; and other castles such as Dover, Southampton, Portland, the Isle of Wight, Fowey, Pendennis, St Mawes, and Falmouth. The castles at the Kentish end of the line were built in a little over eighteen months, but those in Cornwall were not completed until 1545-50. Though often called castles, many of the buildings were in fact defended artillery forts under the command of a governor or master-gunner, and as such are not castles in the true sense of the word. These buildings had the minimum of living accommodation and were designed to make the best use of the modern weapon – the gun. Their armoury ranged from cannons to 6ft-long handguns known as arquebuses. Most of the forts were circular, with the curved walls deliberately designed in this way to deflect cannon balls.

The original building on St Michael's Mount was a priory founded by Edward the Confessor in 1044. When Richard I was away fighting the Third Crusade, the mount was seized for King John by Henry de Pomeroy, although it was subsequently retaken by Richard, who stationed a permanent garrison here. The monks were finally expelled in 1425, and St Michael's became a fortress. It was involved in several rebellions against the Crown; the last was the Cornish uprising against Edward IV.

Right: ST MICHAEL'S MOUNT CASTLE 1908 60984

Right:
RESTORMEL CASTLE
1891 29851

RESTORMEL CASTLE

Photograph 29851 shows the ivy-smothered shell keep and gatehouse of Restormel Castle at a time when the ruin was still a titular possession of the Prince of Wales (it is now in the care of English Heritage). The projecting gatehouse was added about 1100, and the work of replacing the timber palisading with stone occurred some time during the second half of the 13th century. Edmund, Earl of Cornwall, completed the modernisation of Restormel by replacing the internal wooden buildings with stone. The castle was once owned by the Black Prince, son of Edward III, who stayed there occasionally. Restormel is one of the best surviving examples of a medieval shell-keep castle in Britain. Various buildings were ranged around the inner courtyard. The lower floor contained a storehouse, stables and armouries; the upper floor was reached by steps on either side of the gatehouse, and included guest rooms, garderobes (lavatories), bedrooms, small chapels, a solar, a great hall, larder, and a kitchen.

Right: RESTORMEL CASTLE 1931 84140

Left: RESTORMEL CASTLE C1960 R21029

Below: ST CATHERINE'S CASTLE, FOWEY C1955 F43115

ST CATHERINE'S CASTLE

Fowey was once one of the most important ports west of Bristol. In 1346 Fowey was rich enough to contribute 47 ships and over 700 men to Edward III's blockade of Calais. It was still a major port in the 1530s, when it was defended by a chain-link boom and shore battery mounted at St Catherine's Castle.

POLRUAN

This predates Henry VIII's defences by almost 100 years. In 1457 the French launched a raid against Fowey Harbour, and as a result a boom defence was added. There were two towers, one at Fowey and this one at Polruan, and it was between the two that the chain was stretched. The towers mounted small calibre guns, and were designed so that the staircase to the battlements was separate from that between the ground and first floor.

Above: POLRUAN TOWER c1965 P69069

COMPTON CASTLE

Compton Castle, near Marlton, is a 14th-century manor house built without a moat, though the gatehouse came complete without machicolations. Extensive alterations were carried out when Sir Humphrey Gilbert lived here, and in 1808 the estate was sold off in job lots. The castle was bought by a John Bishop, who demolished some buildings and converted what was left into a farmhouse.

Above: COMPTON CASTLE, TORQUAY 1890 25936

DUNSTER CASTLE

Left: DUNSTER, THE MARKET HOUSE AND THE CASTLE 1890 27511

Below: DUNSTER CASTLE 1888 20906

Dunster was held by the Mohun family until 1404, when it was purchased by the Luttrells. In 1645 Dunster was the last Royalist garrison in Somerset, and under the control of Colonel Francis Wyndham it managed to hold out for a siege lasting 150 days. Though ordered to be demolished, Dunster then remained a Parliamentarian garrison for five years, after which the Luttrells were allowed to buy it back. Dunster remained in the Luttrell family until 1737, when it passed by marriage to a Mr Henry Fowles, a descendant of the Mohuns. The Norman gatehouse from the town survives, but most of what we see now is the 1860s remodelling of the castle. Anthony Salvin thoroughly medievalised the buildings to their present romantic appearance. The castle is now in the care of the National Trust.

CORFE CASTLE

Above: CORFE CASTLE FROM THE CHURCH 1897   40318

Left: CORFE CASTLE AND THE VILLAGE 1890   25582

William the Conqueror's original royal fortress guarding the gap in the hills into the Isle of Purbeck was a wooden tower on the motte, which in later generations would form the upper bailey. Quite early on, the motte's defences were improved with the building of a new stone wall around it, and the earliest stone building appears to have been a hall in the western bailey. In photograph 40318 we see the remains of Henry I's great stone tower keep, and to its right is the western bailey where King John built new private apartments. In the foreground is the southern bailey walled by Henry III, and the drum-towered gatehouse built by Edward I. The castle was besieged by Parliament during the Civil War, and was slighted in 1646 on the orders of Cromwell to reduce its strategic importance; the keep and walls were blown up with gunpowder.

A WOMAN DEFENDS THE CASTLE

During the Civil War many aristocratic women turned 'gallant She-Souldiers' to defend their property whilst their husbands were away fighting with the armies. One of the most heroic was Lady Mary Bankes, who in 1643 held Corfe Castle against the Parliamentary forces for six weeks; she personally defended the whole of the upper ward with only her daughters, her waiting gentlewomen, and five men – all of them hurled down stones, boiling water, and red-hot embers so successfully that the besiegers reportedly 'ran away crying'. Eventually the castle was taken, not by force of arms, but by treachery: one of Lady Bankes's men, Lieutenant-Colonel Thomas Pitman, let a group of Parliamentarians into the castle.

Above right: CORFE CASTLE, A GATEWAY 1890 25575

Right: SANDSFOOT CASTLE, WEYMOUTH 1898 41138

The Anglo-Saxon boy-king Edward the Martyr was murdered at Corfe in AD978, allowing his half-brother Ethelred the Unready to succeed; Ethelred's mother has traditionally been suspected of involvement in the crime. King Stephen failed to capture the stronghold in 1139, and the fortress was held by the forces of Simon de Montfort during his conflict with Henry III.

SANDSFOOT CASTLE

Just one mile from Weymouth stand the remains of Sandsfoot Castle. Originally the fort comprised a two-storey building with a north tower and a gatehouse. Now tumbling into the sea, the castle was built by Henry VIII to guard the sea-lanes between Weymouth and Portland. The Tudor topographer Leyland described it as being 'a right goodlie and warlyke castle'. It changed hands several times during the Civil War, before finally falling into ruin in the 1700s.

BERKELEY CASTLE

Above: BERKELEY CASTLE C1955 B72033

Roger de Berkeley, the first tenant after the Norman Conquest, was probably responsible for the construction of the first castle on this site, and we know that Henry I was entertained here over Easter in 1121. The erection of the stone shell-keep began about 1156; it underwent extensive remodelling during the 14th century, when Thomas, 3rd Lord Berkeley, had two of the semi-circular bastions replaced and two others incorporated into the structure of the keep.

At some time during April 1327 the deposed Edward II was brought to Berkeley Castle following his arrest and detainment at Kenilworth. Edward's weak rule and a reliance on favourites rather than experienced men had alienated the barons; even his queen, Isabella, went for a time into exile. Isabella became the mistress of the exiled baron Roger Mortimer, and in 1326 they led an army to England, deposing Edward II in favour of his young son, Edward III. Edward II was incarcerated in Berkeley Castle, then held by Thomas, 3rd Lord Berkeley. The castle was surrendered to John, Lord Maltravers, who set about trying to kill the king; when attempts to bring about his death through starvation and ill-treatment failed, he was murdered.

When the 3rd Lord Berkeley died, his daughter was outraged that her inheritance was to go to a nephew. She sued, and began a family feud that was to last 200 years. Matters came to a head on Nibley Green in 1470, when the rival factions met in armed combat, and Berkeley became the scene of the last private pitched battle on English soil.

THE TOWER OF LONDON

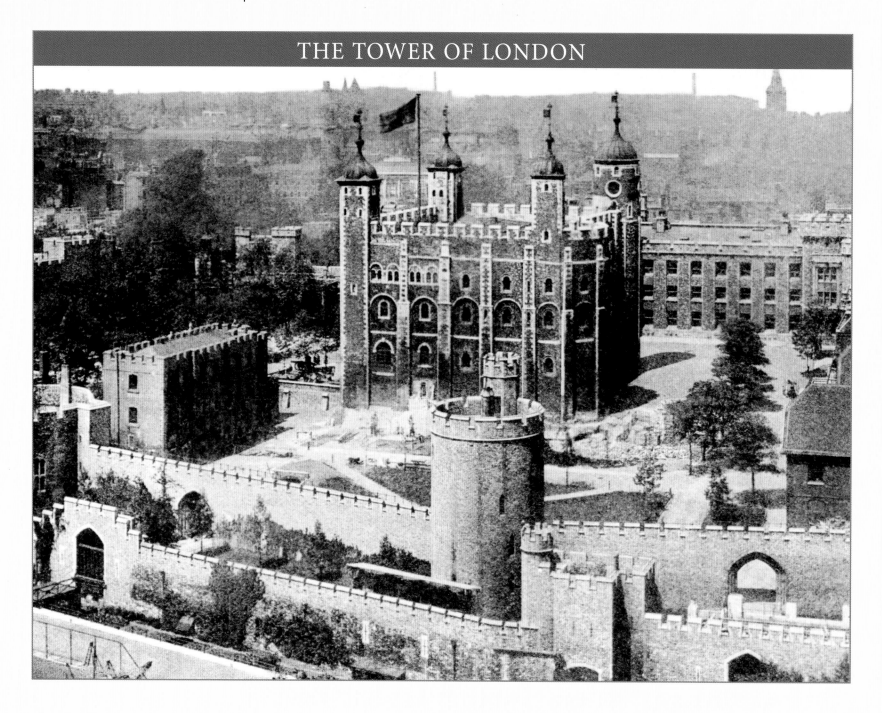

Above: THE TOWER OF LONDON c1890 L130172

In Anglo-Saxon times London was the most important city in England; it had a port, a royal palace and a cathedral. Immediately after the Norman Conquest, William the Conqueror ordered fortifications to be built here. The White Tower was completed in the late 1070s, a formidable structure built to dominate London and to protect the king and his family in times of disorder, functions which the Tower of London has fulfilled throughout its long history.

It was at first defended by the old Roman city walls and by a ditch and rampart; within the enclosure were timber buildings. During the reign of Richard the Lionheart (1189-99) the area covered by the fortress was enlarged by the digging of a new ditch and by the building of a curtain wall and the Bell Tower. Henry III (1216-72) extended the accommodation, improved the great hall and kitchen, and built two towers on the riverfront. Conflict with the barons led him to improve the defences by building a great new curtain wall and nine new towers and constructing a new moat. Henry's son Edward I (1272-1307) further demonstrated royal authority over London by spending the huge sum of £21,000 on additional defences; his son Edward II used the Tower regularly as a refuge during his turbulent reign.

By now the Tower housed the Royal Mint; it was also used to store official papers and the Crown Jewels, and the king's menagerie was also housed here. After the Wars of the Roses, when the Tower had been considered an important asset to those seeking power, more stable times came with the Tudors. From now on the Tower's main function was as a prison (prisoners executed here included Anne Boleyn, Thomas More and Archbishop Laud). It ceased to be a royal residence in the 17th century; the Tower of London has now entered a phase of glorious retirement as a museum and tourist attraction.

Left: THE TOWER OF LONDON 1890 L130071

Above: THE TOWER OF LONDON, MARTIN TOWER C1930 L130270

WINDSOR CASTLE

Windsor Castle is the world's oldest inhabited castle, and it is the principal residence of the sovereigns of the United Kingdom. Windsor is thought to have been built by William the Conqueror. This first castle consisted of a large motte, on top of which was built a timber tower protected by palisades; the motte divided the Upper and Lower Wards. However, though Windsor Castle is thought to date from around 1070, the earliest written record of it is the entry in the Domesday survey of 1086. When Windsor was besieged by the Dauphin of France in 1216, part of its defences were still wood and earth; in 1221 its castellan Engelard de Cigogne was authorised to begin a series of works to repair the siege damage and upgrade the fortress. It was Edward III who was responsible for the present-day plan of the castle. At a cost of £50,000, between 1358-68 he reconstructed and transformed it from a fortress to a royal palace (in 1377 it was the largest palace in England). St George's Hall and the Norman gateway are also his.

Above: WINDSOR CASTLE, THE HENRY VIII GATE 1914 66985t

Right: WINDSOR CASTLE,
THE NORMAN GATE AND THE MOAT GARDEN 1914 66993

ST GEORGE'S CHAPEL AND THE ORDER OF THE GARTER

The present St George's Chapel was started during the reign of Edward IV in 1475. When he died, Edward IV was buried in the chapel, which was eventually completed in 1528 during the reign of Henry VIII. (It is one of the finest examples of late Gothic or Perpendicular architecture in the country, and is the resting place of ten sovereigns, including Henry VIII, who is buried next to Jane Seymour.) It was against the background of the age of chivalry in 1348 that Edward III founded the Most Noble Order of the Garter, the world's oldest order of chivalry. Founded in Windsor (where he was born) the order consisted of 24 special knights, plus the Prince of Wales and the king (26 in total), and this has not changed throughout the centuries. Each knight has a stall in St George's Chapel where their knightly achievements hang (crest, helm, mantling, sword and banner). The order's motto, 'Honi Soit Qui Mal Y Pense' – 'Shame on him who thinks ill/evil of it' – probably refers more to the leading topic of the day, Edward's claim to the French throne, than the romantic tale concerning a lady's garter! Since 1348 there have been almost 1,000 Knights of the Garter, chosen by the ruling monarch of the day. In Edward's time they would have been real knights in armour, a select group of top fighting men who had shown their valour fighting the French during the Hundred Years' War. Today people are chosen who have served their country, such as Baroness Thatcher, the first woman Prime Minister, or who have achieved something exceptional, like Sir Edmund Hilary, the first man to scale Everest.

WINDSOR CASTLE, ST GEORGE'S CHAPEL 1895 35394

WINDSOR, CASTLE HILL
1906 53719P

GUILDFORD CASTLE

The ruinous 70ft-high 12th-century keep is all that remains of Guildford Castle, which was built partially on top of an earlier Anglo-Saxon fortification. The only action the castle ever saw was in 1216, when it was occupied by the French at the invitation of the barons rebelling against King John. The castle was essentially a 'pleasaunce', a place for relaxing and pleasure. Set in beautiful countryside with good hunting, half way between the new capital, London, and the coast, the castle became very popular with the kings of England.

The locality particularly took the fancy of Henry III, and during his long reign of over 50 years (1216-1272) he returned again and again to it. In the building accounts of the improvements that he made to the castle, the usual bald estimates are developed at some length, which implies that Henry knew exactly what he wanted and was determined to get it. The royal family was to be decently housed on their visits to the town. There was to be a special chamber for the young prince, Edward, 'with proper windows well-barred', the queen was to have an entire new wardrobe 'with a chimney and private chamber and window equal in width to the two existing windows ... with two marble pillars and close it with glass windows between the pillars', and she was to have her own private garden. Elsewhere in Henry's castle the luxury of glass, both plain and coloured, made its appearance. The great hall was to be fitted up 'with white glass lights with the picture of a certain king sitting on a throne and a certain queen likewise sitting on a throne'.

An arch from the outer gateway of the castle still stands in Quarry Street.

Above: GUILDFORD CASTLE 1895 35064p

Left: GUILDFORD CASTLE, THE GATEWAY 1895 35065

CARISBROOKE CASTLE

Above: CARISBROOKE CASTLE AND
THE OLD MILL c1955 C26035

Carisbrooke Castle on the Isle of Wight stands on a high mound, dominating the town below. The site may have been fortified as long ago as Roman times, though much of today's castle dates back to the Norman period, with later additions. The foundations for the castle were laid by William FitzOsborne, a kinsman of William the Conqueror. The most impressive feature is the gatehouse, which mostly dates from the 14th century. In 1377 the French landed on the Isle of Wight; they failed to take the castle, which was ably defended by Sir Hugh Tyrell, Lord of the Island. The castle repelled the enemy's repeated attempts to storm it, and French morale was weakened when part of the enemy force was cut to shreds in an ambush on the castle approaches, and then when the Lord of Stenbury, Peter de Heyno, famed for his deadly accuracy with the crossbow, felled the French commander. The slit from which he is said to have taken aim with his legendary 'silver bow' is still visible on the west wall of the castle – it is known as Heynoe's Loope, a relic of a true Island hero. The result was stalemate - the castle could not be taken, and the French could not be turned back. In the end, the dispute was settled by cash, the raiders agreeing to go home in exchange for a hefty lump sum, officially recorded as a fine. Following the threat from Spain in 1588, the Italian fortifications engineer Federigo Gianibelli was commissioned to improve Carisbrooke's defences; his curtain wall and bastions are still in very good condition.

THE FATE OF THE NODDIES

The track on which French soldiers were reputedly ambushed during the siege of Carisbrooke in 1377 became known as Deadman's Lane. It is in the area of Newport known as Nodehill, which itself recalls the abusive term 'Noddies' used by 14th-century Islanders when referring to idiots – or Frenchmen! Admiral Lord Nelson's victory at Trafalgar in 1805 led to the lane's being renamed Trafalgar Road.

ISABELLA DE FORTIBUS

CARISBROOKE, THE WINDOW OF ISABELLA DE FORTIBUS c1880 C26301

At the end of the 13th century the Isle of Wight's two-and-a-half centuries of semi-independence under private ownership was ended. The very final holder of the Lordship was actually a lady: Isabella de Fortibus was the last of the ruling dynasty begun by the first Richard de Redvers. She has been described as beautiful, formidable, intelligent and energetic. A one-word summary would be – remarkable. She was widowed at the age of 23, and was just 25 when the death of her brother Baldwin propelled her to unexpected power at Carisbrooke as the Lady of the Wight. Despite this unpromising start, the Countess Isabella ruled the Island with an astonishing degree of toughness for the next 30 years. She made enemies, largely by being over-fond of litigation, and, while granting freehold and privileges to the developing boroughs, she was in more or less constant dispute with abbeys, towns and other major institutions on either side of the Solent. Isabella was a woman alone in a society otherwise totally dominated by men, and her 30-year reign was no mean achievement. But relationships between England and France were deteriorating. Edward I feared invasion, and the Isle of Wight was an obvious stepping-stone for a full-scale onslaught against the mother country. Newtown's deep-water harbour might be a key factor in terms of both invasion and defence. Unsure of the support he might receive on the Island from Isabella de Fortibus, Edward snapped up the Manor of Swainston, of which Newtown still formed part, completing the purchase following a visit to the Island in 1285. It seems not to have been enough for the jittery monarch. So, when Isabella fell seriously ill, Edward seized his chance to act decisively. The Countess's son, Thomas, had died at the age of 16, leaving her without direct heirs. On her deathbed in 1293, Isabella was persuaded by King Edward's officials to sign over the Isle of Wight, in exchange for a relatively paltry sum of money, to the English Crown, in whose hands it has remained ever since.

Above: CARISBROOKE, CASTLE HILL 1908 60509

Charles I was held prisoner at Carisbrooke from November 1647 to the autumn of 1648, before his transfer to the mainland and his trial and subsequent execution. A window through which he attempted to escape is still shown to visitors. Princess Elizabeth, second daughter of Charles I, never left the Isle of Wight once she had been taken there in August 1650. This extraordinarily gifted girl, who could read in French, Italian, Latin and Hebrew at just eight years old, was fourteen when she arrived at Carisbrooke with her little brother, Henry, Duke of Gloucester, following initial banishment elsewhere, with Parliament fearing that the continued presence of the children in London might re-ignite Royalist sympathies. Their mother and elder sister had long since left the country for Holland, and their brother, the future Charles II, had also escaped Cromwell's clutches. When the children reached Carisbrooke, they were effectively orphans. By all accounts, they were treated with respect and kindness at Carisbrooke, but Elizabeth's always fragile health failed her completely on the Island. Already suffering from rickets, she contracted pneumonia after being caught in a shower on the castle's bowling green. On the morning of 8 September, the young princess was found dead in her bed. Her coffin was placed in a vault inside the original St Thomas's Church. A brass plate made for a former minister was reversed, inscribed and fixed in place. And that, miserably, was that. Eventually, at the time of the present church's construction in the 19th century, an appalled Queen Victoria put right that final indignity by commissioning a magnificent sculptured monument above the re-located tomb. It stands at the head of the church's north aisle. In a touching gesture, Victoria ordered that the windows on the north wall near the monument should be fitted with stained glass so that only a gentle light should fall on the tragic princess's tomb.

PORTCHESTER CASTLE

Above: PORTCHESTER CASTLE 1898 42708

The original Norman fort at Portchester was merely a corner of the 3rd-century Roman Saxon Shore fort, defended on its two open sides by the building of a wooden palisade. Portchester is a formidable piece of Roman military engineering even today. Its massive walls are 10ft thick and were originally over 20ft high. They enclose an area of nine acres. A series of hollow D-shaped bastions project from the curtain walls. They were probably all floored originally at parapet level to support an artillery piece, most likely a ballista. Such platforms were a relatively new phenomenon and, in this fortress, built to defend anchorage and hinterland, we have the first of the remarkable series of defensive positions built in the Portsmouth area over the next almost two thousand years.

The Roman military occupation of the site ceased cAD370, but there is evidence that in the last years of the Roman era the site was occupied by, and gave some protection to, a small civilian population who may well have cultivated the area inside the fort. These were very uncertain times. The Picts and the Scots were attacking Britain from the north and the Saxons were attacking in the south. By the early 5th century, Rome had virtually cut all links with Britain and left the country to fend for itself.

It was after the rebellion against Henry I by his elder brother Robert Curthose that the decision was made to build a castle proper. The tower keep, which when built was only one storey high, has walls 12ft thick, and when two further floors were added it was similar to those at Norwich and Corfe. By the end of the 12th century, the Norman castle in the inner bailey was complete. It was used regularly by Henry II on his journeys between England and Normandy. It was at Portchester in 1164 that Henry received the Bishop of Evreux on his mission to mediate between the king and Becket. The king was at Portchester again in 1172 on his way to France to plead his innocence of any complicity in Becket's death before the papal legates. Important prisoners were confined at Portchester, and treasure was sent regularly from Winchester to Portchester for shipment to Normandy.

ARUNDEL CASTLE

The fine old market town of Arundel is dominated by its castle, which is now the home of the Dukes of Norfolk. The castle was originally established by a Norman baron, Roger de Montgomery, to guard the gap in the South Downs cut by the River Arun and to defend the coast against possible French raids. The original castle, raised in about 1068, comprised a 70ft-high motte and two baileys, built on the site of an earlier Anglo-Saxon fortification. Robert de Beleme is thought to have begun the building of the circular stone shell-keep; the work continued under Henry I and Henry II after Arundel had become a royal fortress. Badly damaged during the Civil War, Arundel has undergone a considerable amount of rebuilding. It was transformed into a Gothic pile during the Napoleonic period, and rebuilt yet again in the 1890s when the then Duke of Norfolk employed the architect Buckler to build him a medieval-style castle, so most of what we see here is Victorian mock medieval.

There are various family portraits in Arundel's castle, some of them dating back to the Wars of the Roses of the 15th century. The Norfolks have lived at Arundel since the 16th century. According to a plaque at the bottom of the High Street, 'Since William rose and Harold fell, There have been Earls at Arundel'.

Above: ARUNDEL CASTLE AND THE TOWN FROM THE AIR c1955 A62001

Below: ARUNDEL CASTLE 1906 56725t

Above: ARUNDEL CASTLE, THE LIBRARY 1898   42521

A HARSH PUNISHMENT

In 1292 the Earl of Arundel was excommunicated by the Bishop of Chichester for walking his dog in the Bishop's forest; this was because the nobility of England and France jealously protected their game reserves, and established 'forest law' to protect the animals they liked to hunt.

HASTINGS CASTLE

The ruins of Hastings Castle are believed to stand on the site where William the Conqueror built his first castle in England; this would have been a wooden, prefabricated structure shipped over with his invasion force. The present ruins date from the 11th and 12th centuries.

Above: HASTINGS CASTLE 1925 77965

BODIAM CASTLE

Above: BODIAM CASTLE 1890 25390

Below: BODIAM CASTLE 1902 48239

The town of Bodiam is located on the River Rother, and was once a port that shipped iron ingots and cannon which were made in the area. Bodiam Castle was constructed in 1385 because of the imminent threat of invasion by the French, and was the last castle to be built in England for coastal defence. A licence to build Bodiam Castle was granted to Sir Edward Dalyngrigge, 'to make a castle thereof in defence of the adjacent country against the King's enemies'. The moated castle was restored by Lord Curzon in the early 20th century. The original approach was along a wooden bridge at right angles to the castle walls, thus exposing an attacker's unshielded flank to fire from the defenders. Details are difficult to make out in this pre-restoration photograph, but in front of the gateway tower is the ruined barbican, and in front of that is the much overgrown octagonal island, which at one time might also have been fortified. Bodiam was protected by three drawbridges, two fortified bastions, three portcullises and an internal arrangement of rooms and doorways designed for defence.

LEEDS CASTLE

Above: LEEDS CASTLE 1892 31499

Right: LEEDS CASTLE c1955 L29003

Originally a wooden Saxon fortress built on two islands, the building was transformed into a solid stone castle at the end of the 12th century by the Norman baron Robert de Crevecoeur. Leeds Castle served as the dower home for a number of medieval queens, and it was a favourite haunt of Eleanor of Castile (wife of Edward I), Catherine of Valois (wife of Henry V), and Henry VIII.

The Leeds Castle Foundation was established in 1974 to preserve the place as a 'living' castle through income generated from visitors, conferencing and special events.

HEVER CASTLE

Hever Castle was built in the 13th century, and in the 16th century was owned by the Boleyn family, whose daughter Anne became the second wife of Henry VIII. This photograph shows it in 1891, in good condition but reduced to nothing more than a farmhouse. Hever was rescued from obscurity by William Waldorf Astor, who bought it in 1903 and spent a fortune restoring it to its former glory.

Left: HEVER CASTLE 1891 29396

SALTWOOD CASTLE

There was a fortification here in the late 5th century, possibly on a Roman site; it was replaced in the 12th century by a Norman castle, which was altered over the next 200 years. In 1580 it was destroyed by an earthquake, but it was restored in the 19th century. It was from Saltwood Castle, near Hythe, that four knights set off one winter evening in 1170 for Canterbury to murder Thomas à Becket. King John granted Saltwood to the Archbishops of Canterbury, but it was returned to the Crown by Archbishop Cranmer in the 16th century. In more recent times it was the home of Sir Kenneth Clark, the art historian, and his son, the historian and MP for Kensington and Chelsea, Alan Clark (1928-99), whose diaries became bestsellers. His book 'The Donkeys' (1961) was a savage assault on British military ineptness during the First World War.

Above: SALTWOOD CASTLE 1890 25896

DOVER CASTLE

Henry II's great keep at Dover stands high above the mural towers of the inner bailey. It was under Henry and his son Richard I (the Lionheart) that Dover was transformed into one of the strongest and most impressive fortresses in Britain. This was one of the first concentric castles in the kingdom, nearly 100 years ahead of any others. The massive, cube-shaped great tower has walls 17-21ft thick, and two rings of walls surround it. The inner bailey was defended by fourteen flanking towers, and the outer by twenty, and both gates had barbicans. The castle was besieged by Prince Louis of France in 1216, but it held out, even though the north gate was successfully mined. The threat of invasion from France, and later from Spain, meant that Dover's defences were kept in a good state of repair and upgraded when necessary.

Above: DOVER CASTLE, THE KEEP FROM THE WALLS 1890　25705

Left: DOVER CASTLE, CONSTABLE'S TOWER AND GATE 1890　25707

In an inner courtyard tower there is a well over 300ft deep; near the wellhead are two lead pipes that were once connected to a cistern from which water was pumped to various rooms in the castle. In the 13th century an outwork was made towards the northern high ground, and a large round tower was built in the ditch between the outwork and the castle. To enable sallies to be made to the rear of an attacking force, an underground passage was cut through the chalk to link the castle, tower and outwork – the passage was made high and wide enough for a mounted, armed knight to ride through.

ROCHESTER CASTLE

A wooden castle at Rochester was hastily thrown up by the Normans in the early period of their conquest, and later this temporary structure was replaced by a stone fortress. Bishop Gundulph of Rochester, who had previously organised the building of what we now call the Tower of London, was in charge of this project. Starting in 1078, and using surviving Roman walls as a foundation, Gundulph built a stone curtain wall, which to this day marks the boundary of Rochester Castle. A huge stone keep, 70ft square and 113ft high from the ground to its battlements was added later. Building work commenced in the late 1120s, using Kentish ragstone to construct the walls, which were up to 12ft thick. Cement was made with mud from the River Medway. The embedded remains of shellfish can still be seen by the sharp-eyed visitor.

Forced labour from Rochester and its satellite villages would have done much of the work, although specialist craftsmen were probably brought in from other parts of Britain – or even from the continent. The main access to the castle complex was through a gateway overlooking the cathedral and walled town. This entrance was approached by a drawbridge (later replaced by a stone causeway), which lay across the moat surrounding the castle. Today's Esplanade did not exist, and at high tide the River Medway lapped against the castle's outer walls.

It is easy to overlook the fact that most castles did not see much military action. Rochester's fortress only saw trouble when the Norman ruling élite, or their successors, the Anglo-Normans, fought among themselves. Substantial damage was not only done in 1215, when besiegers managed to bring down the south-eastern corner of the keep, but also during later civil wars in 1264. Repairs were carried out in a defensively more effective, rounded style, the results of which can be seen today.

Sir Thomas Wyatt's Kentish followers, protesting against Queen Mary's Spanish marriage in 1554, secured Rochester Castle before their march on London. Similarly, Parliamentary troops were sent to seize it in the early days of the Civil War in 1642. However, as time passed, the Weldon family, to whom James I had sold the castle in 1610, began to sell off stone and timbers from the castle, and the fabric of the fortress, by then redundant, deteriorated.

Above: ROCHESTER CASTLE FROM THE RIVER C1865 2514p

Above: ROCHESTER CASTLE 1906
53728

PIGS BRING DOWN THE KEEP TOWER

The tower at the south-eastern corner of the keep at Rochester Castle is rounded, whereas the others are rectangular. This is a result of King John's siege of the castle in 1215, after Archbishop Langton had refused to surrender the fortress to the Bishop of Winchester. During the siege, the king's forces dug a tunnel underneath the tower, supported with pit props. They filled it with brushwood and the king ordered 'forty of the fattest pigs of the sort least good for eating to bring fire beneath the tower'; the brushwood was set on fire, and the fat in the pig carcases increased the power of the blaze. All the timbers in the tunnel caught fire and collapsed, bringing down the tower.

WARWICK CASTLE

Above: WARWICK CASTLE 1892 30998

At the Peace of Wedmore in AD878 between the Danes and the Anglo-Saxon King Alfred, the two sides agreed to split the country into two areas of control. The Danes were allowed to settle in the Danelaw where Danish laws, not Anglo-Saxon, were followed. The earliest fortifications at Warwick were thrown up cAD915 by Ethelfleda of Mercia, the daughter of Alfred the Great who, with her brother Edward the Elder, attempted to conquer the lands of the Danelaw. The ditch and palisade defences were placed round the town itself, Warwick at this time being little more than a frontier town next to the Danelaw. It was Henry de Newburgh, one of Henry I's councillors, who built a large wooden motte and bailey on the site of the present castle; he may well have replaced his wooden keep with a stone-built keep before his death in 1123, and either he or his son replaced the palisading with a stone wall. By 1263 the castle was in the hands of William Maudit, who supported Henry III during the Baron's War; Warwick Castle was sacked and all but destroyed by forces loyal to Simon de Montfort. When Maudit died in 1268 the castle passed to the Beauchamp family, who set about its complete rebuilding.

Warwick Castle's fortifications are mainly the work of the Beauchamps. Two great towers dominate: Caesar's Tower, which was begun in about 1345 by Thomas Beauchamp, and Guy's Tower, which was built by Beauchamp's son, another Thomas, around 50 years later. Caesar's Tower has no connection with Julius Caesar, or any other Roman emperor. It was originally named Poitier's Tower, after the Bishop of Poitiers, who was captured during the Hundred Years' War. His ransom paid for the tower, situated at the bottom of Mill Street.

The castle's defences were formidable. In addition to the towers and curtain walls built by the Beauchamps, it possessed a moat, drawbridge, barbican and portcullis, followed by a long passageway to the inner courtyard. Attackers trying to get from the outer to the inner gateway faced an almost suicidally hazardous task. Photograph W31301 shows the portcullis of the castle. Should any attacker pass through the first portcullis, he would find another one behind. At the same time he would face a lethal crossfire of missiles, including those dropped or shot through the holes in the ceiling; these weapon slits are well named as 'murder holes'. Such attackers were often referred to as 'the forlorn hope' as they had little chance of surviving.

Few castles can have had so much influence over national events as Warwick. For part of its history, Warwick Castle was in royal hands, but even when it was not, it played a part in national events. At the time of Richard Neville 'the Kingmaker' in the 15th century it was the most powerful centre in the country, except for the royal court. Earl Richard was known as 'the Kingmaker' because of the power and influence he wielded during the struggle between the houses of York and Lancaster known as the Wars of the Roses. The Duke of Clarence, brother of Edward IV, built the Boar Tower and Clarence Tower of Warwick Castle, before joining the Earl of Warwick in rebellion against the king. He ended his days in the Tower of London, drowned in a butt of malmsey wine, according to Shakespeare in 'Richard III'.

The builders of Warwick Castle recognised that a cliff overlooking a river was the ideal site for a defensive stronghold, and they took full advantage of it. However, the south front would not originally have looked as it does today: the façade is largely a Victorian creation, having been restored in 1863-66, and again in 1871 after a major fire. Bought by the Madame Tussaud's Group in 1978, Warwick Castle has now become a hugely popular visitor attraction. Warwick Castle holds several interesting and historic items in its collection, including a helmet said to have belonged to Oliver Cromwell, and a sword said to have belonged to the legendary hero Guy of Warwick.

WARWICK'S GHOSTLY DOG

Warwick Castle is said to be haunted by a ghostly Black Dog. Local legend says it is the transmogrified spirit of Nell Bloxham, who was forbidden by the Earl of Warwick to sell milk and butter from her cottage at the foot of the castle walls.

Above: WARWICK CASTLE, THE PORTCULLIS c1900 W31301

The Cedar Drawing Room in Warwick Castle, the largest of three drawing rooms, takes its name from the ornate cedar-wood panelling. Like all the staterooms, it was restored after the Civil War, probably around 1670. It has outstandingly rich decoration and furnishings, including three Van Dyck portraits, five Waterford chandeliers, an Aubusson carpet and a unique red-and-white marble mantelpiece by Robert Adam.

Left: WARWICK CASTLE, THE CEDAR DRAWING ROOM c1900   W31303

Below: KENILWORTH CASTLE 1922   72405p

KENILWORTH CASTLE

Above: KENILWORTH CASTLE 1892 30935

The first castle to be built at Kenilworth is thought to have been a motte and bailey constructed between 1122 and 1127 by Geoffrey de Clinton. It was de Clinton's son who built the keep in 1162. A century later, Kenilworth was involved in the Barons' War between Henry III and a rebel group of barons led by Simon de Montfort. In 1266, rebel forces were besieged in the castle for six months - the longest siege in English history. The keep survived that, but it was unable to withstand the assault of Oliver Cromwell in 1642. By the end of the Civil War, Kenilworth was in a poor state. It was given to a group of officers who divided up the land between themselves, drained the lake, and dismantled several towers.

One of the prisoners kept in Kenilworth during its long history was the deposed Edward II, who was held here before his transfer to Berkeley Castle, where he is believed to have been murdered. It was John of Gaunt, one of the powerful sons of Edward III, who set about transforming Kenilworth from a Norman fortress to a Gothic palace. Work began around 1389, with only the keep being retained. The entire inner ward was rebuilt; it included a great hall, private apartments, kitchens and storerooms. However, it was Robert Dudley, Earl of Leicester, who completed the process two centuries later after Elizabeth I gave her favourite the castle in 1563. He remodelled the old apartments and added an extensive range of imposing new buildings. On the left of photograph 72405p is Leicester's gatehouse, which had been converted into a private dwelling by the time this view was taken. In 1937 Kenilworth was donated to the nation by Sir John Siddeley.

KIRBY MUXLOE CASTLE

Above: KIRBY MUXLOE CASTLE c1965 K126004

Begun by William, Lord Hastings in 1480, and never finished, Kirby Muxloe is an early example of the use of brick in castle building. Although equipped with loops for handguns (they are the openings that look like inverted keyholes), Kirkby was intended to be more a country house than a fortress. The surviving west tower is where Jane Shore, mistress of Edward IV, came after the king's death.

NEWARK-ON-TRENT CASTLE

Above: NEWARK-ON-TRENT CASTLE 1895 35551

Right: NOTTINGHAM CASTLE FROM THE CANAL 1890 24699

Alexander, Bishop of Lincoln and lord of the manor of Newark, replaced the original timber fortress here with one of stone, employing Ranulph of Durham to build the gatehouse; Newark thus became one of the finest castles in 12th-century England. King John died at Newark Castle on 19 October 1216. His body was embalmed and taken to Worcester, where it was buried in the cathedral at the king's own request. Following the castle's surrender to the Parliamentarians at the end of the Civil War, it was ordered to be slighted so that it would be of no further military value. Slighting, however, was carried out to varying degrees: Nottingham Castle was all but destroyed, but at Newark the three-storey gatehouse, three towers and the curtain survived. This photograph shows the north-west wall of the ruined castle towering above the River Trent.

NOTTINGHAM CASTLE

Following the Norman Conquest in 1066, William Peverel erected a castle on Tower Rock at Nottingham. It was a naturally impregnable site, with towering cliffs on two sides, and the castle dominated the country around, including the main road north, which crossed the River Trent below. The castle was steadily added to over the years, and its walls were rebuilt from 1068 onwards. From the mid 12th century it was an important royal castle, and in the 1470s it acquired grand state apartments in the middle bailey. In 1212 King John hanged 28 Welsh boy hostages from Nottingham Castle walls during a Welsh rebellion. During the brief reign of Richard III, Nottingham Castle was the king's principal residence, and thereafter the great tower which he had completed was known as Richard's Tower. Richard III called the castle his 'Castle of Care'. This name does not, as popularly supposed, reflect the king's melancholy view of the castle, but quite the opposite – a modern rendering might be 'the castle of his regard and care', as he was very fond of Nottingham Castle. In 1485 Richard III rode out of his Castle of Care to the battle of Bosworth Field, where he lost his crown – and his life. This battle saw the end of the Plantagenet line, and the beginning of the new Tudor dynasty, under the victor, Henry VII.

Charles I raised his standard at Nottingham Castle in 1642, the first action of the Civil War, although he soon left the town, which was strongly pro-Parliament. After the war the castle was left ruinous.

In the 17th century what remained of Nottingham's castle was given to the Duke of Newcastle, who had the upper and middle baileys cleared and levelled in order to build himself a ducal palace. Completed in 1679, after the Duke's death, the palace appears as austere as a prison block from a distance, but more ornamented when seen from a closer viewpoint. The building became a natural focus of resentment locally, and was sacked and burnt out in 1831 when Nottingham's outraged citizens learned that the Duke of Newcastle had voted against the Great Reform Bill. Eventually the ruin was taken over by the town and restored as a museum, which opened in 1878 as the first Museum of Fine Art in England outside of London.

Left: NOTTINGHAM CASTLE
1890 22845

The bulk of the medieval castle, largely made a ruin by the Civil War, was 'slighted', or made useless, by order of Parliament in 1651. Now only the outer bailey east walls and a 14th-century gatehouse survive. Photograph 22843p shows it in poor condition prior to being drastically restored in the late 19th century, which unfortunately took away a lot of its character. A small amount of the original old stonework can still be seen in the archway and at the foot of the right-hand tower.

Right: NOTTINGHAM CASTLE,
THE GATEHOUSE 1890 22843p

MORTIMER'S HOLE

It was at Nottingham Castle that the young Edward III trapped his mother, Queen Isabella, with her lover, Roger Mortimer, and created one of the castle's most popular and enduring legends - the story of Mortimer's Hole. This was supposed to be a cave leading from the cellars of Ye Olde Trip to Jerusalem Inn to the castle, through which Edward III crept to capture Mortimer, who was later put to death. Mortimer's ghost is reputed to haunt the cave.

NOTTINGHAM, YE OLDE TRIP TO JERUSALEM INN 1920 69430

COLCHESTER CASTLE

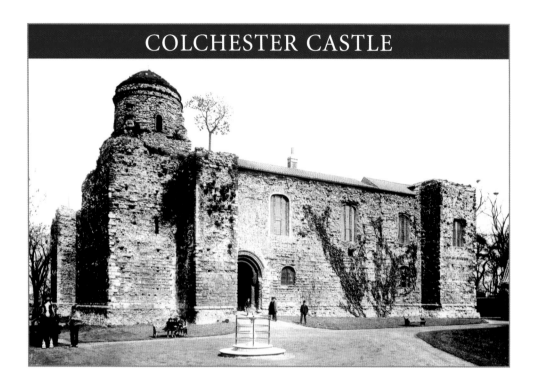

Colchester had the largest castle keep ever built in Europe. Constructed in 1080, its floor plan is half as big again as the White Tower of the Tower of London; indeed, the keep's resemblance to the Tower of London's White Tower is striking, and some believe that it was built by the same designer, Gundulph, Bishop of Rochester. It was erected around the podium of the Roman temple to the God-Emperor Claudius. The temple was dedicated to the emperor's victory in the Roman invasion of Britain of AD43; it was destroyed during the rebellion of Boudicca cAD60. Originally the keep was 91ft high with more storeys, so now it appears much squatter and less menacing than when it was first built. However, although the number of storeys of the castle was reduced in the 1680s, it is still imposing. It now houses a museum of Roman artefacts, including a terracotta baby's feeding bottle dating from about AD180. There are also some touching terracotta toys in the shape of a boar, a bull and other animals, which were found buried in a baby's grave.

Colchester Castle had a turbulent history: in 1216 it was even captured by the French forces that were aiding the barons in their rebellion against King John. By 1250 it was being used as a prison; it held Protestants during the reign of Queen Mary, at least fifteen of whom were burned at the stake, and during the reign of Elizabeth I it held Catholics. It also played a key role in the eleven-week siege during the Civil War, before the Parliamentary army retook it from the Royalists. In the late 17th century it was sold to John Wheely, who partly demolished it for its materials. The castle became a prison again in the 18th century, and then a museum. In 1892 the castle grounds were opened as a public park, and in 1920 Viscount Cowdray bought the park and the castle and gave it to the town.

Top: COLCHESTER CASTLE 1892 31524

Above: COLCHESTER CASTLE, THE WALLS AND THE TOWN HALL 1907 57536

NORWICH CASTLE

Above: NORWICH, THE CATTLE MARKET AND THE CASTLE 1891

28177

At the time of the Norman Conquest, Norwich was both an important town and a major port. Control was quickly established with the erection of one of the earliest motte and bailey castles in England. A stone keep was built by Henry I, but the one seen in this photograph is the result of much rebuilding, inside and out. The Norman castle at Norwich was built at the highest spot in the town: this involved destroying a large number of Saxon houses and at least one church. The castle keep – a cube almost 30m (95ft) deep and 23m (70ft) high – is the largest in England apart from the Tower of London. The bailey, or outer defence, stretched over the area now known as Castle Mall, down to the Steam Packet, and included the site of the Royal Hotel, and also the area covered by shops on both sides of the street now called Castle Meadow.

In 1883 the castle keep was offered to the county authorities, who waived their right in favour of the city. There was keen debate as to how the castle should be used. Some people thought the modern buildings around the old keep should be pulled down, the area turned into a public park, and the keep itself allowed to decay into a 'romantic ruin'. The alternative idea – to use both the keep and the surrounding buildings for a museum – prevailed.

KETT'S REBELLION

Norwich in 1549 was where 'Kett's Rebellion' broke out. In fact, it was not a rebellion at all but an outburst of non-violent protest by the poor and the lower middle class. Several thousand people camped out on Mousehold Heath, at the top of what is now Gas Hill. They were eventually crushed by Swiss mercenaries under the Earl of Warwick. The battle took place at a site called Dussindale. It is not certain where this was. Evidence suggests that the battle was fought on Mousehold Heath, probably in the Long Valley to the north of Gurney Road. Kett was captured and hanged from the keep of Norwich Castle. The city ordered that a local holiday be established celebrating Kett's downfall: all the shops in the city were to close on 27 August 'from henceforward forever'! Attitudes to the rebellion have changed over the centuries: on the 400th anniversary of Kett's death a plaque was put up at the castle in his honour.

Built by William de Albini in the 12th century, Castle Rising sits inside a ring-work, with a small bailey on either side; these defences may originally have been constructed of wood. The richly decorated keep, one of the largest in Britain, is built from local stone, and contains a great hall, a chapel, a kitchen, a chamber and a combined buttery and pantry.

Below: CASTLE RISING 1898 40894

CASTLE RISING

TATTERSHALL CASTLE

Above: TATTERSHALL CASTLE 1893   32081

Tattershall was extensively rebuilt by Ralph Cromwell, a veteran of the battle of Agincourt and Lord Chancellor of England. It was built entirely of brick, an early use of the material on such a large scale, with windows and dressings of Ancaster limestone. Today, little survives of Tattershall save for its magnificent five-storeyed tower keep. On the top of the keep is a double fighting platform; Ralph had copied the very latest French practice by building machicolated parapets. Tattershall was rescued from becoming derelict by Lord Curzon, who refurbished it between 1911 and 1914.

BOLSOVER CASTLE

Above: BOLSOVER CASTLE 1902 48905

Here we see the ruins of the once luxurious state rooms of Bolsover Castle. It was probably in these rooms that the Duke of Newcastle lavished thousands of pounds on entertaining Charles I. One such three-day visit by the king in 1634 is said to have set the duke back £15,000, a phenomenal amount of money in 17th-century England.

The death of Henry I in 1135 saw England torn apart by civil war. The succession had been settled by Henry on his only surviving legitimate heir, his daughter Matilda, but the throne was seized by her cousin Stephen, a grandson of William the Conqueror. As well as being harassed by Matilda's supporters, the north of England was also sorely troubled by Scots raiding parties. In 1137 the English inhabitants and the Norman garrison of Clitheroe Castle joined forces to fight off one such raid. Much later, during the Civil War, in 1649 Clitheroe was reduced on Cromwell's orders so that it would be of little, if any, strategic importance. In 1660 it was given, along with the Honour of Clitheroe, by Charles II to General Monck. Monck had fought for Parliament, but had later been one of the prime movers in bringing about the restoration of the monarchy.

Below: CLITHEROE CASTLE 1927 80535

CLITHEROE CASTLE

Right: LANCASTER CASTLE, THE GATEWAY 1896 37369

The first castle at Lancaster was built by Roger de Poitou, though the massive stone keep was added around 1170. King John lavished money on Lancaster, building curtain walls, round towers, and Adrian's Tower (also known as Hadrian's Tower), now much altered. In 1322 Robert Bruce sacked the town, but was unable to take the castle. Lancaster Castle was, in theory, the residence of the lord of the Honour of Lancaster. John of Gaunt's son, the future Henry IV, built the impressive gatehouse and flanking octagonal towers around 1400 (37369), and to a large extent it took over the role of the keep. It was built of stone salvaged from earlier structures, and equipped with a portcullis and machicolations, and is still the main entrance. It was Henry's estates that became the Duchy of Lancaster, which have belonged to the Crown ever since.

At the top of Lungess Tower or the keep of the castle is 'John o'Gaunt's Chair', which rises a further 10ft higher. This was the beacon tower of the castle, which was used both for warning beacons and celebratory ones, such as for coronations. At the time of the approach of the Spanish Armada, the beacon on 'Gaunt's embattled pile' was seen on Skiddaw in the Lake District, warning of the danger to England. John of Gaunt himself visited Lancaster in 1385 and 1393 for a total of nine days, and they were the only times he came in his life.

Lancaster itself did not particularly take sides during the Civil Wars, but the town was of strategic importance, thanks to its castle and also its position on a major north-south route, together with the crossing of the Lune. It also had great symbolic value as the county town. It is odd that although there were Royalist supporters further up the Lune valley, neither the castle nor the town were garrisoned by them in 1642. As a result, in February 1643 a company under Sergeant-Major Birch came up from Preston and took the surrender of the castle for the Parliamentarians. This was not the end of the Royalist cause. The Earl of Derby then decided it was important that his forces should retake Lancaster; he set out from Wigan on 13 March, possibly having decided to do so because of the wreck of a Spanish vessel off Rossall Point in the Fylde – its 22 cannon had been taken to Lancaster Castle. On the way to Lancaster he added to his numbers by gaining troops from the Fylde. He arrived on 18 March, entering the 'Towne of Lancaster several waies' and meeting very little resistance, for the Parliamentary troops had retreated into the security of the castle. As a result, the town was open to plunder and burning. Penny Street in particular suffered, its timber and thatch buildings soon being set ablaze, the garrison having abandoned them to their fate. It is estimated that 90 premises were lost; in 1645 Parliament made a grant of £8,000 as compensation for them. Later in the war, a 'rude company of Yorkshire Troopers', whom even the Parliamentarians admitted were a problem, garrisoned the castle. After the Civil War it was decided to demolish the castle so that it could not be garrisoned, but to retain those parts used for the courts and the prison. This left the gatehouse and the buildings on the south and west sides. Much damage must have been done to the castle, for it was estimated that repairs would cost nearly £2,000 when a return to military usage was proposed in 1664.

A QUAKER IN PRISON

George Fox, the founder of the Quaker movement (the Society of Friends), came to Lancaster and preached in 1652. He was persecuted for his religious beliefs, and imprisoned in Lancaster Castle. The prison part of the castle must have been in as poor a condition as the military part. The evidence for this is George Fox's description of it during his imprisonment in 1664. He was put into a tower where the smoke of the other rooms came up so thick as to stand like dew on the walls; sometimes the haze was so great that he could hardly see his own burning candle. The under-jailer could hardly be persuaded to come up to unlock one of the upper doors above him when the smoke was thick, owing to his own fear of it. Rain fell upon Fox's bed, and although he tried to stop it up, in the winter his shift would be 'as wet as muck with the rain that came in upon me'. Where he was held was high, so that as fast as he stopped up the hole, the wind would blow it out again. Fox lay in these conditions all winter until the next Assize Court. As this description does not match any of the present building, it is thought that Fox was held in a tower that has now been demolished.

Whilst the bridle at Lancaster Castle shown above was used to punish gossips, it was also used on Quaker women to stop them preaching. The bridle was very heavy to wear. A bar went into the victim's mouth to hold down her tongue and prevent her from speaking.

Above: LANCASTER CASTLE, THE GOSSIPS' BRIDLE (THE BRANK) 1927 80517

Left: LANCASTER CASTLE, A CASTLE WARDEN ON JOHN O'GAUNT'S CHAIR 1927 80507p

PEEL CASTLE

Above: PEEL, THE TOWN FROM THE CASTLE 1893 33045

Left: PEEL CASTLE, THE ROUND TOWER 1893 33052

The castle on St Patrick's Isle at Peel dates from between c1098 and 1103, when Magnus Barefoot built a timber fort there. The bulk of the surviving fortifications date from the time of Thomas, 1st Earl of Derby, and were constructed between 1460 and 1504 as a defence against Scottish raiders. A few years ago a 9th-century woman's grave was excavated on St Patrick's Isle. Although in a Christian cemetery, she had been buried with grave goods: comb, knife, chatelaine, spit (for roasting) and a goose wing (used for brushing out an oven). The most spectacular item, however, was a necklace with a wide variety of beads representing all areas of the known Viking world: a chain of memories rather like a souvenir charm bracelet.

Built in the Irish style, the round tower at Peel Castle dates from the 10th or 11th centuries and would have been used as a place of refuge during raids by pirates or Vikings. It is built from local red sandstone and stands 50ft high. Originally it would have had a conical stone roof, but this was replaced by the crenellated top many centuries ago.

CASTLE RUSHEN

Above: CASTLE RUSHEN, CASTLETOWN 1897 39894

Left: CASTLE RUSHEN, CASTLETOWN 1893 33021

The present Castle Rushen dates from the 12th to the 14th centuries. It was here in 1265 that Magnus, last of the Isle of Man's Norse kings, died. With his death began nearly 70 years of Scottish rule until the island was taken by Edward III of England. When William Montacute, Earl of Salisbury, was appointed First Lord of Man he chose Castletown for his capital. Montacute strengthened the fortress defences, adding a new tower on the eastern side and a twin-towered gateway. Later 14th-century improvements included a curtain wall and the heightening of the keep. The glacis was added by Cardinal Wolsey c1540 while he was serving as a trustee for the under-age Earl of Derby.

In 1312 England was on the brink of civil war. Robert Bruce seized the advantage by dispatching his brother Edward, together with James Douglas, into northern England. They sacked a number of towns, including Durham and Hartlepool, while Robert reduced England's Scottish possessions to a handful of fortresses. In 1313 Robert invaded the Isle of Man, besieging and almost destroying Castle Rushen in the process.

Above: CASTLE RUSHEN, CASTLETOWN c1885 C47501

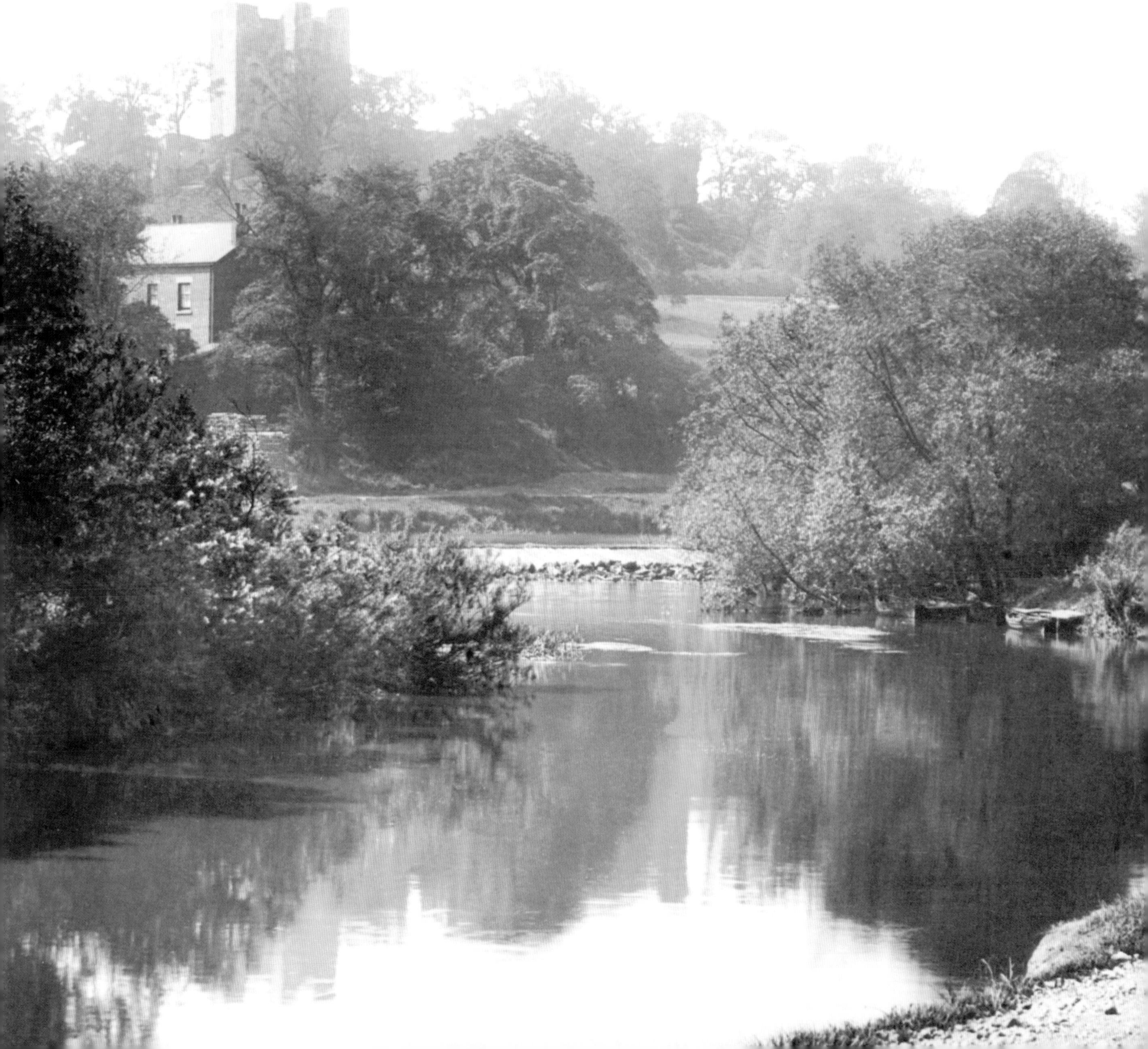

CONISBROUGH CASTLE

This great fortress was built by Hamelin Plantagenet, half-brother of Henry II. The round keep is thought to be the first of its type to be built in England; it was designed to be difficult to mine and resistant to attack with a battering ram. The keep is supported by six wedge-shaped buttresses which rise higher than the keep to form turrets. Though the buttresses served no useful purpose in propping up the keep, they did fulfil certain functions. One contained two cisterns for water drawn from a well beneath the keep; another housed an oven; yet another contained an oratory, and another a pigeon loft.

CONISBROUGH,
THE CASTLE FROM THE RIVER 1895

35317A

Above: CONISBROUGH CASTLE 1895 35318

Left: PONTEFRACT CASTLE, THE KEEP 1964 P155035

PONTEFRACT CASTLE

The ruined keep in the south-west corner of Pontefract Castle dates from the mid 13th century, when it was rebuilt in a polygonal form similar to those at Knaresborough, Southampton, Roxburgh and Warkworth. During the Civil War the castle was held for the king, changing hands once before being recaptured by the Royalists. It finally fell in 1648 after a siege lasting six months, and orders were issued for it to be slighted. Demolition took place between March 1649 and August 1654; some material was salvaged for repairs to Hull Castle.

An important part of any castle was the kitchen area and its associated service rooms. These were often built on stone-vaulted floors as a precaution against fire, and most kitchens boasted more than one oven. The butchery of animals for the pot usually took place in the outer ward.

Left: PONTEFRACT CASTLE, THE KITCHENS 1964 P155036

SIEGE WARFARE ARTILLERY WEAPONS

The trebuchet, introduced to Britain in the 13th century, was an effective and relatively accurate siege engine. There were many variations in its design, but basically it consisted of a long arm pivoting on an axle. The shorter end of the arm carried a counterweight (lead, or containers of earth or rubble), and the longer end the projectile in a sling. Winches pulled the long arm down, and when it was triggered, the force of the counterweight let it fling the projectile. The range could be adjusted by another, sliding counterweight on the arm. Stones weighing up to 300 pounds could be thrown up to 500 yards, with terrifying and devastating effect. The mangon, or mangonel, was powered by torsion: one end of its long arm went through a skein of ropes or leather strips, which were twisted by capstans. The other end was winched down, loaded with the projectile, and released by a trigger mechanism. As the arm hit a horizontal bar, it released the projectile. The mangon's range was probably about 200 yards. The ballista was a siege engine like a very large bow, powered by the springiness of the bow; it shot heavy arrows or stones. The springald or springal, as its name suggests, was also powered by springiness. It threw a heavy dart or lance by flexing a board, rather in the same way as flicking pellets with a ruler. Petraria is the general name for all these weapons. Cannon were probably first used in the 14th century, and at that time they were as dangerous to their users as to the enemy. This was because their makers did not yet have the technical expertise to forge them in one piece, so that they were likely to explode. Technical advances in the 15th century allowed much larger and more efficient cannons to be forged, like Mons Meg at Edinburgh, but the older styles of weapons continued to be used into the 16th century.

KNARESBOROUGH CASTLE

Above: KNARESBOROUGH CASTLE c1873 6662

Left: KNARESBOROUGH CASTLE, THE GUARD ROOM 1914 67277

A Norman castle was built here by Serlo de Burg, but the ruins we see are from a later period. During the reign of King John, Knaresborough served as a royal arsenal for the manufacture of quarrels, the missiles fired from crossbows. The word probably derives from the French 'carreau', meaning 'diamond-shaped, faceted' – these missiles had a four-sided sharply pointed metal head, which could cause considerable damage to buildings and fearsome wounds. The phrase 'to pick a quarrel' derives from the crossbow-man's choosing the best weapon against a particular target. Knaresborough Castle was extensively rebuilt in the 14th century under the lordship of Piers Gaveston, Edward II's favourite and possibly his lover.

The town of Richmond owes its origins to its spectacularly defensive site high above the River Swale. This commended it to Count Alan Rufus of Brittany, kinsman of William the Conqueror, who built the castle c1071 as the prestigious headquarters of an immense area of feudal land-holdings later known as the Honour of Richmond. Most early Norman castles were motte and bailey earthworks, but Richmond was one of the first stone-built castles in the country. In addition to the triangular Great Court there was a smaller east court, the Cockpit, and a large outer bailey, now the present Market Place. The magnificent keep, almost 100ft tall, which was added by Conan, Duke of Brittany in the second half of the 12th century, is a superb example of Norman military architecture.

The ruined castle was a major attraction during Richmond's Georgian heyday. Its owner, the Duke of Richmond, created a fashionable promenade, Castle Walk, around it. The castle was leased to the North York Militia in 1854, and several new military buildings were erected shortly before the outbreak of the Crimean War. The castle is now in the guardianship of English Heritage, who commissioned a Contemporary Heritage Garden for the outer court known as the Cockpit.

RICHMOND CASTLE

Above: RICHMOND CASTLE AND THE BRIDGE 1893 32275t

RICHMOND, THE CASTLE
FROM THE GREEN 1898 41642

Left: RICHMOND CASTLE, THE KEEP 1908 59493t

Above top: MIDDLEHAM CASTLE 1893 33130

Above: MIDDLEHAM CASTLE c1960 M70095

MIDDLEHAM CASTLE

Above: MIDDLEHAM,
THE VIEW FROM THE CASTLE C1955 M70074

The castle at Middleham was originally a motte and bailey. The stone keep was built in 1170, with the stone curtain walls and improved living quarters being added shortly afterwards. The castle eventually passed into the hands of the Neville family, and in 1471 Richard, Duke of Gloucester, came here to be tutored by the Earl of Warwick. Richard later married Warwick's daughter Anne, and their son Edward was born at Middleham in 1473; he also died there in 1484. Anne herself died soon afterwards, and Richard, by then Richard III, met his end on Bosworth Field in 1485.

The original entrance was from the eastern gatehouse across the moat; the present entrance is a grand three-storey northern gatehouse. The lofty keep is about 66ft high; it had two wells and two stone tanks for keeping live fish in the kitchens on the ground floor. The keep also provided exceptionally large living quarters, well protected by three well-guarded gates and an anteroom.

BOLTON CASTLE

Above: BOLTON CASTLE, CASTLE BOLTON
1911 63473p

Left: BOLTON CASTLE, CASTLE BOLTON,
THE MUSEUM 1911 63481

This castle was built by Richard, Lord Scrope some eighteen years after being granted a licence to crenellate by Richard II. Though similar to Bodiam Castle in shape, and designed with a well-defended entrance that featured no less than five doorways and a portcullis at either end, Bolton's principal function appears to have been residential; it was one of the first castles to have chimneys. Mary, Queen of Scots was imprisoned here for six months, and the castle was partially dismantled at the end of the Civil War. The castle was later used by local families, who lived in tenements built within the walls.

Below: BOLTON CASTLE, CASTLE BOLTON 1911 63477

SCARBOROUGH CASTLE

The building of Scarborough Castle began around 1135. The castle was the scene of the first action by the barons against Edward II in the 14th century. At that time the castle was held by Piers Gaveston, Edward's despised favourite. The siege was led by the Earl of Lancaster, but Gaveston held out until forced by starvation into surrendering. Despite being promised safe conduct to London, Gaveston was seized and taken to Warwick Castle, where he was held prisoner before being summarily beheaded, an event which shocked many people even in those brutal times. This photograph shows the approach to the castle, which was by way of a narrow causeway, and the remains of the keep that once stood 100ft high with walls 12ft thick.

Right: SCARBOROUGH CASTLE 1890 23475

Lying alongside the Roman fort of Brovacum, Brougham Castle dates from the 12th century and was held by the Veteripont and later the Clifford family. The licence to crenellate was granted in 1397 – the castle was considered important in the defence against Scottish raids, and indeed in 1420 it was laid waste by the Scots. James I was entertained here lavishly in 1617 as the guest of Francis, Earl of Cumberland and his son Henry Clifford. In 1648 during the Civil War the castle was captured by the Parliamentarians, who then used it as a quarry, partially demolishing the place and selling off the stone. In 1651 the castle was restored by the redoubtable Lady Anne Clifford, who died there in 1676.

Artists and writers have celebrated the castle ruins and their setting, notably J M W Turner and William Wordsworth. Turner's evocative and atmospheric study made in 1809 was used for his 'Rivers of England' series of 1825. Wordsworth recalled pleasant childhood hours spent exploring the buildings, linking them with the name of Sir Philip Sidney, an ancestral relative of the castle's restorer, Lady Anne Clifford.

BROUGHAM CASTLE

Above: BROUGHAM CASTLE, PENRITH 1893 32938

SIEGE ENGINES

A siege engine was a wheeled wooden tower which could be relatively easily moved to wherever it was needed. It usually had several storeys from which bowmen could shoot at the castle garrison; it could also carry a catapult. Sometimes at the top was a bridge which could be dropped on the castle wall to facilitate an assault, and at the bottom a battering ram. During the siege of Stirling in 1304-05 Edward I employed no fewer than seventeen siege engines. He spent a large sum of money on a new engine, nicknamed 'the war wolf', and he wanted to test it. After the surrender of the castle, Edward ordered part of the garrison to remain in the castle while he tried out his new engine, which virtually destroyed the gatehouse. The condition of the men who were at the receiving end of this bombardment was not recorded.

Moveable Tower with Bridge and Battering Ram.

The earliest castle here is thought to have been built by Bernard de Baliol; it consisted of a ring-work with wooden palisading protected by an outer ditch defence. When John Baliol was crowned King of Scotland in 1292, his English estates, including Barnard Castle, were declared forfeit to the English crown. The Bishop of Durham claimed Barnard, and actually occupied it from 1296 to 1301, when Edward I took it back and eventually gave it to Robert Clifford. Over the next 200 years or so, the Bishops of Durham disputed ownership of the castle with whoever was in residence.

Below: BARNARD CASTLE AND THE RIVER TEES 1898 41432

BARNARD CASTLE

DURHAM CASTLE

Together with the cathedral, the castle at Durham is now designated a World Heritage Site. The strategic importance of Durham became evident after the Norman invasion of England in 1066. The old Saxon defences were replaced, and a more sophisticated stronghold was founded beside the minster in 1072 by orders of William I. Initially the castle consisted of a timber stockade on an earthen mound, but by the end of the century the stronghold had been fortified and a bailey built around the level ground to the west. Over the years a succession of Prince-Bishops have added important sections to the great building. In the 1930s a huge rescue operation had to be carried out to underpin the subsiding foundations; while the cathedral was built on solid bedrock, the castle was built on less substantial material.

To the left of photograph 30759 is the entrance to the 100ft-long Great Hall of Durham Castle, built during the reign of Bishop Bek. Bishop Cosin's impressive Black Staircase (see 30763) stands in the angled tower between the Great Hall and the 12th-century building of Bishop Pudsey. Completed in 1662, the staircase was freestanding, even though it rises through four floors, and is one of the most impressive staircases of its time in the country. It is 17m high and, with the exception of the intricately carved softwood side panels, is made from oak. In later years the staircase had to be supported with columns owing to a substantial increase in downward weight caused by the building of an additional room on the top storey. The mixture of architectural styles and the work of individual bishops can be identified by the coats of arms which are placed in conspicuous places on the walls, including those of Bishop Cosin, Bishop Pudsey, Bishop Trevor and Bishop Tunstall. A university was officially established at Durham in 1657 during the Commonwealth, but it was suppressed following the Restoration. Durham was finally granted its university in 1832. In 1835 Bishop van Mildbert exercised one of his few remaining powers as a Prince-Bishop by turning over the castle to the university, and the keep was reconstructed in 1840 to provide student accommodation.

Above: DURHAM CASTLE 1892 30759

Below: DURHAM CASTLE, THE BLACK STAIRCASE 1892 30763

Above: Durham Castle, Tunstall's Gallery 1918 68218

Above Right: Durham Castle, The Norman Arch 1892 30762

Bishop Tunstall's gallery leads from the first landing of the Black Staircase. The inner hall of this gallery was formerly the outer wall of Bishop Pudsey's hall, and the great round-headed doorway seen in 30762 which faces the gallery's largest window was once the principal entrance to the lower part of this 12th-century building, which stands directly opposite the castle gatehouse. It was probably approached under a canopy by a long flight of steps from the courtyard. The doorway is in near immaculate condition, and is believed by many to be one of the finest examples of late Romanesque stone carving in England.

NEWCASTLE UPON TYNE CASTLE

Above: NEWCASTLE UPON TYNE CASTLE 1901 N16322p

The original New Castle on the Tyne was built by Robert Curthose, the brave but short-tempered and headstrong eldest son of William the Conqueror, on his return from campaigning against Malcolm III of Scotland. It was a motte and bailey: a wooden tower on a mound was protected by a ditch on its west side and by precipitous banks on the other three, and it was from this fortification that Newcastle would derive its name. This castle was replaced by the present castle between 1172 and 1177. In 1812 Newcastle's castle was bought by the Corporation, and it was after this date that the corner turrets and battlements were added to the keep. The Black Gate was originally constructed in 1247, when the castle's defences were upgraded, but the house on top of the gate is a much later addition.

This has been a fortified site since the 6th century, when it was the residence of the Northumbrian kings. King Oswald was the first Christian king to live here, and he was so admired and respected by St Aidan of Lindisfarne that Aidan once grasped the king's hand, saying: 'Never let this hand consume or wither'. When Oswald was later killed in battle his hand was cut off and revered as a sacred relic in Bamburgh church, apparently remaining uncorrupted. The Norman keep with its four corner turrets, similar to that at Rochester, was built between 1164 and 1170, and was besieged by William II (William Rufus) in 1095. Unable to take the fortress from Robert de Mowbray, 3rd Earl of Northumberland, William headed south, leaving the prosecution of the siege to others. Mowbray attempted to escape, but was captured. His wife only surrendered Bamburgh after her husband had been paraded before the walls under threat of having his eyes torn out. Following an eventful history, the medieval buildings of Bamburgh Castle were in ruins when they were sold to the Bishop of Durham, Lord Crewe, in 1704. In 1757 a trustee of the Crewe estate began restorations. The castle was further restored in the late 19th and early 20th centuries.

BAMBURGH CASTLE

Above: BAMBURGH CASTLE AND THE VILLAGE C1955 B547022

THE STORY OF THE LAIDLEY WORM

An old story associated with Bamburgh Castle is that of the Laidley Worm. Long ago one of the Northumbrian kings at Bamburgh remarried in his old age, not knowing that his new wife was a witch. The new queen was jealous of the king's daughter, and turned her into a dragon, or 'worm'. This dragon ravaged the surrounding countryside and terrified the inhabitants. The king's son, the Childe of Wynde, who was overseas, heard of the dragon and returned to Northumbria intending to kill the monster and restore peace to his father's kingdom. When the wicked queen heard of this she sent her imps to raise storms and sink the ship, but they had no power over the vessel, for its keel was made from the wood of the protective rowan tree. The Childe landed safely and approached the dragon with drawn sword, not knowing that the monster was actually his sister. But even through her enchantment the princess recognised her brother and refrained from attacking him. Instead, the voice of the girl came through the dragon's jaws, saying:

'O, quit your sword, unbend your bow,
And give me kisses three;
For though I am a poisonous worm,
No harm I'll do to thee.

O, quit your sword, unbend your bow,
And give me kisses three;
If I'm not won ere set of sun,
Won never shall I be.'

Recognising his sister's voice, the young man bravely kissed the dragon three times. The spell was broken and the princess stood before him where the dreadful dragon had been. After she had explained how the spell had come about, the Childe entered the castle, where he found the wicked queen cowering in her bower. The Childe struck her with a twig of the magical rowan tree, and turned her into an ugly toad with huge bulging eyes. The toad croaked and hopped away, and is said to live still in a cave below the castle.

A Tudor fort sitting on top of Beblowe Crag, Lindisfarne was raised for defence against the Scots. Construction began in 1542 and was completed by 1550, using stone salvaged from the ruined Benedictine priory. The only action the castle ever saw was when it was 'captured' from its garrison of just seven men by two Jacobites; they managed to fly their flag for a few hours before they were thrown out. The castle was demilitarised in 1819, and in 1902 it was converted into a private residence for Edward Hudson, editor of 'Country Life', by Sir Edwin Lutyens.

Right: HOLY ISLAND (LINDISFARNE), THE CASTLE c1940 H348112

HOLY ISLAND (LINDISFARNE)

CHEPSTOW CASTLE

The original castle at Chepstow was begun by William FitzOsbern in 1067. The site chosen was a long narrow ridge high above the River Wye. FitzOsbern built a long rectangular fortified hall (the Great Tower) on the narrowest part of the ridge. A two-storey structure, it features pilasters and a string course of re-used Roman tiles, and its walls are only 3-6ft thick - keep walls are usually between 8-20ft thick. FitzOsbern protected his hall by means of a stone curtain wall on all four sides; the defensive capability of the three landward sides was enhanced by a ditch.

Left: CHEPSTOW CASTLE FROM THE BRIDGE 1893 32495

THE REGICIDE HENRY MARTEN

Marten's Tower, and its flanking turrets, was erected between 1285 and 1293 by Roger Bigod III. The tower is a massive D-shaped structure protected at ground level from attack either from battering ram or undermining by two spur bastions. The tower performed a dual function. Militarily, it enabled flanking fire to be directed against attackers attempting an assault upon the barbican and twin-towered gatehouse. Domestically, it formed the private apartments of Roger Bigod. Marten's Tower is named after the regicide Henry Marten (1602-80), who was imprisoned in fairly comfortable conditions here for twenty years until his death in 1680. Marten had been one of the signatories to the death warrant of Charles I, and as such faced almost certain death himself at the Restoration of Charles II. His life, however, was spared. This might have been due to the fact that after the king's execution, the ultra-Republican Marten had become convinced that Oliver Cromwell wanted to be crowned king himself; this led to a serious rift between the two men, and Marten became an outspoken opponent of the Lord Protector and all his works.

CHEPSTOW CASTLE, MARTEN'S TOWER 1893   32498

RAGLAN CASTLE

In the 1460s William Herbert set about remodelling Raglan in the contemporary French style, designed to take into account the latest thinking in military architecture; Raglan was primarily a fortress, not a stately home. These features included a tower-keep separated from the rest of the castle by its own moat, multi-angular towers, and ornate machicolations of the type seen in 54519t adorning the tops of the hexagonal corner towers of the gatehouse. The circular gun-ports at the base of the gatehouse walls are obscured by hedging. As a professional soldier, William Herbert had fought for and been knighted by Henry VI. It was, however, his unwavering support for Edward IV at the battle of Mortimer's Cross in 1461 that earned him the title of Baron Herbert. Other honours were to follow. In 1462 he was created a Knight of the Garter, and in 1468 he was created Earl of Pembroke as his reward for taking Harlech Castle and capturing both Jasper Tudor and his nephew Henry (later Henry VII).

Left: RAGLAN CASTLE 1906   54519t

Raglan was not divided into wards but into two courts, the Stone and the Fountain. These are in turn separated from one another by what was a 60ft-high building that included the great hall, the earl's private dining room, a large buttery, a withdrawing room, and the great gallery. The Fountain Court (32532) housed the castle's state apartments. During the Civil War Charles I visited Raglan after his defeat at the hands of the New Model Army at Naseby on 14 June 1645, arriving on 3 July from Abergavenny. The king was still at Raglan on 22 July when he received the news that Goring had also been defeated at Langport by Fairfax and Cromwell, signalling the beginning of the end for the Royalist cause.

Right: RAGLAN CASTLE, FOUNTAIN COURT 1893 32532

Below: RAGLAN CASTLE 1893 32533

NEWPORT CASTLE

Above: NEWPORT CASTLE 1893 32631

Founded in 1172, the castle at Newport was heavily rebuilt during the 14th and 15th centuries. This photograph shows the surviving curtain wall facing the River Usk. In the centre is the square gate tower with its arched water gate. Boats could enter the castle through the water gate, as there was a small quay to the rear of the tower. Double gates controlled the water level under the tower, and unwelcome visitors trying to gain access by this route would have to get through two portcullises.

CRICKHOWELL CASTLE

Above: CRICKHOWELL CASTLE 1893 32609

Crickhowell Castle lies twelve miles south-east of Brecon. Originally it was a motte and bailey with a timber keep, and belonged to the de Turberville family. When rebuilt in stone it featured both a shell-keep and a shell gatehouse.

Many academics scoff at Cardiff Castle, claiming that with its diversity of styles and influences it is not a true castle; however, it has a 1,900-year-old history of repelling invaders. What makes it unique is that it is the combined work of many building periods, from Roman right up to Victorian renovations. The Romans erected a wooden fort on this site in the 1st century, and later the first Norman castle was built in about 1091 by Robert FitzHamon, Lord of Gloucester, as a motte and bailey fortification, probably on top of an earlier Welsh stronghold; the Normans later replaced it with a stone castle, and extra defensive height was achieved by piling the spoil on the top of the circuit walls to create a rampart. In 1106 Robert Curthose, Duke of Normandy, waged an unsuccessful war with Henry I; the defeated duke was taken to Cardiff Castle, where his eyes were put out, and he remained a prisoner until his death in 1134. In the medieval period a moat was a necessity, but in later years it was filled in. When the famous landscape gardener 'Capability' Brown was commissioned by the 1st Marquess of Bute to landscape the grounds in the 1760s, he re-opened the moat to make an ornamental lake. The ruined stone Norman keep stands on the motte (or mound) of the earliest castle that was built soon after the Norman Conquest, and is exceptionally well preserved. Ringed by its own moat, and steeply stepped, it sat within the castle grounds serving as a second line of defence from marauders and invaders.

CARDIFF CASTLE

Above: CARDIFF CASTLE 1893 32672

Left: CARDIFF CASTLE, THE SOUTH SIDE 1893 32670

The wealth of the Bute family, creators of the Cardiff docklands, was displayed loud and clear in the 19th century when the 3rd Marquess of Bute, reputedly the richest man in the world in his day, commissioned the opium-smoking genius William Burges to transform his residence into a no-expense-spared medieval fantasy palace decorated with astonishing detail. This folly of all follies can still be seen in all its glory, for medieval banquets now take place here, and remains a monument to the wealth that was created by the Welsh coal miners.

During the Civil War, the Lord of Cardiff, the 5th Earl of Pembroke, was a Parliamentary sympathiser, but most of the gentry of Glamorgan were Royalist. Cardiff Castle was taken and occupied by a Royalist garrison. However, by the time of the Royalist defeat at the battle of Naseby in 1645, the Welsh were no longer willing to support the king's cause. Charles I sought refuge at Cardiff Castle, but help was refused him, and most of South Wales passed into the hands of Parliament. The king observed: 'The hearts of the people of Wales are as hard and rocky as their country.'

GHOSTS AT CARDIFF CASTLE

Cardiff Castle is the subject of several ghostly tales. The spectre of the 2nd Marquess of Bute, who began the restoration of the castle, is said to appear sometimes; he walks through the library fireplace, then passes through a thick stone wall into a corridor, and then through the wall of the chapel, finally ending his journey in the room in which he died in 1848. Another blurred, ghostly shape has also been seen in a stockroom of the castle, where items get mysteriously disarranged; the dining hall also suffers unexplained manifestations, with lights flashing on and off, and heavy doors apparently being opened and shut by an invisible hand.

ST DONATS CASTLE

There are no identifiable remains of the castle built here in the 12th and 13th centuries. St Donats was rebuilt by Sir William Stradling during the reign of Edward III and remodelled during the Tudor period. The castle is divided into two wards, the outer being defended by a gatehouse with a portcullis. Photograph 87913 shows the approach to the gatehouse by way of a bridge over the dry ditch defence. A number of Stradling family members fought for Charles I during the Civil War, including Sir Edward Stradling, who commanded a Welsh regiment at the battle of Edgehill (23 October 1642), where he was captured. St Donats was ordered to be slighted in 1646, but was restored to the family in 1660, when Grinling Gibbons was commissioned to supply carvings for the state rooms. The castle underwent further restorations in the 19th century. The south front of St Donats overlooks the Bristol Channel, and a series of terraced gardens leads down to the shore.

The last of the male line of the Stradling family died in 1738, not of old age in his bed, but killed in a duel at Montpellier whilst on the Grand Tour. The young man's body was brought back to St Donats, where it lay in state in the great gallery, looked down upon by the portraits of his ancestors. Unfortunately, the funerary decorations caught fire, and his body, the portraits and the great gallery went up in flames.

Opposite: ST DONATS CASTLE
1937 87913

Right: ST DONATS CASTLE
1937 87914

Below: ST DONATS CASTLE,
THE TUDOR GARDENS
1910 62537

CAERPHILLY CASTLE

Above: CAERPHILLY CASTLE c1955 C5122

Along with Windsor and Dover, this vast fortress is one of the largest castles in Britain, and covers over 30 acres. Dating from the 13th century, it is not just a monument in stone; the water defences are equally impressive. Gilbert de Clare's second attempt to build a castle at Caerphilly got under way in 1271, his previous unfinished castle having been destroyed by Llywelyn in 1268. This castle too was attacked by Llywelyn; this forced Henry III to intervene and declare Caerphilly neutral territory. However, de Clare had the backing of the barons and retook his own castle by force, causing the Welsh to withdraw. The construction of Caerphilly and its associated water defences must have been a drain on resources, even for a man as wealthy as Gilbert de Clare; his income has been estimated as being in the region of £5,550-£6,000 a year, and the construction of the castle probably cost between £7,500-£11,000.

Photograph C5122 shows Caerphilly Castle following the restoration both of its fabric and its water defences by the Marquess of Bute. The principal residential block, which included the great hall, was situated along the south side of the inner curtain wall. The drum towers at the angles of the inner curtain were also used for accommodation, and the constable's apartments were in the east gatehouse. In the centre of the curtain of the outer ward is the south water gate; there might also have been one on the north side, but no trace now remains. The wall going off to the right of the photograph is part of the fortified dam.

Caerphilly Castle is said to be haunted by the shade of a green lady, who moves from turret to turret, as well as by ghostly soldiers. Some staff have reported smelling a strong scent of perfume in the flag tower for no obvious reason. Caerphilly Castle has a tipsy leaning tower, probably caused by an attempt to blow it up during the Civil War; the degree from the perpendicular is greater than that of the Leaning Tower of Pisa.

Situated two miles south-south-west of Bridgend, Ogmore was originally a ring-work with a timber palisade built around 1116 by William de Londres to guard the crossing points of the Rivers Ewenny and Ogmore. The stronghold formed an integral part of the defences of the western border of Glamorgan, which also included the castles of Newcastle at Bridgend and Coity.

Below: OGMORE CASTLE, BRIDGEND 1901 47908

OGMORE CASTLE

SWANSEA CASTLE

Above: SWANSEA CASTLE 1893 32724

The Normans recognised the strategic importance of the Swansea area. In 1106 Henry de Beaumont, Earl of Warwick and newly appointed Lord of Gower, arrived; by 1116 he had built a castle on a small knoll near the river, a timber and turf structure defended by a system of ditches and banks. In 1116 a Welsh army rampaged through Gower and attacked the castle; they were fended off, but in 1192 the castle was besieged for ten weeks. The castle was again attacked in 1215 and 1217, and in the later attack the castle was destroyed. In about 1330 Bishop Henry de Gower built a castle – or rather a fortified house – at Swansea. It was severely damaged in the early 15th century by the Welsh freedom fighter Owain Glyndwr, and was demolished by the Parliamentarians in 1647, during the Civil War. All that is left today is the large tower and some domestic buildings. The River Tawe once flowed under its walls, but it was eventually re-routed to make way for the modern harbour and other developments. Much of High Street, Wind Street and St Mary's Church would have been within the outer castle wall.

OXWICH CASTLE

Top: OXWICH CASTLE 1910 62598

Above: OXWICH CASTLE 1935 O38011

The original castle on this headland was built by Philip Mansell, but in 1541 Sir Rhys Mansell (1487-1559) built a large manor house within the remnants of the old building. It even incorporated a part of the curtain wall, gatehouse and great tower. Above the gate can be seen the arms of Sir Rhys, who by the reign of Queen Mary had become one of Glamorgan's chief landowners. His son Edward later brought Oxwich Castle up to date with a long gallery and great windows. Oxwich was Sir Rhys's main residence. He was certainly a man of his time; he was a veteran of the wars in Ireland, Chamberlain of Chester, and a member of the Council in the Marches. Between 1542 and 1546 he served in the wars against France and Scotland. Though he appears to have been out of favour during the reign of Edward VI, he returned to prominence upon the accession of Queen Mary with his appointment as chamberlain and chancellor for the south of Wales.

At Christmas 1557, Oxwich was the scene of an incident that resulted in litigation before the Court of the Star Chamber. Sir Rhys was distantly related to Sir George Herbert, another wealthy landowner and Vice-Admiral of the Crown. The trouble started over a cargo of a French merchant ship wrecked at Oxwich Point. Sir George intended to hold an enquiry to access ownership of the spoils, and sent two retainers ahead to secure the cargo. They had no warrant, so Sir Rhys's tenants refused to hand anything over. The whole episode got out of hand, and ended in the death of Anne Mansell, who had ridden over to Oxwich with the intention of acting as the family peacemaker.

OYSTERMOUTH CASTLE

Situated four miles south-west of Swansea overlooking Swansea Bay, Oystermouth Castle is one of the most intact castles in Gower. The name derives from a Norman/ English corruption of Ystmllwynarth. The first stronghold on the site was probably built by Henry de Beaumont, Earl of Warwick, following his being made Lord of Gower by Henry I. After its destruction in an uprising in 1287, Oystermouth was rebuilt as a courtyard castle. At one end was a three-storey gatehouse whose top floor was occupied by a large chapel. At the other end was the rectangular tower, the remains of which are the subject of photograph 32739. The two structures were linked together by a high curtain wall. Remodelling went on into the 16th century. In the 1690s, Isaac Hamon wrote: 'There is in this parish a very spacious castle having many dry Roomes, vaults and sellers in it, with staires, towers and walkes very firm, in some arches there are flowes and coates of arms painted in divers colours'.

Below: OYSTERMOUTH CASTLE 1893 32739

Below: PENNARD CASTLE 1893 32760

PENNARD CASTLE

Pennard stands high above a tidal creek some eight miles west-south-west of Swansea. The ruins are of a late 13th-century rectangular castle built on the site of an earlier stronghold. There is a twin-towered gatehouse to the landward side, and square towers at each corner of the curtain wall. There is little information as to who owned Pennard, or even lived in it. There is no evidence for any 15th- or 16th-century rebuilding work, so the castle might well have been abandoned during the 14th century.

LLANSTEFFAN CASTLE

Llansteffan is a double enclosure castle of the 12th and 13th centuries. Its defences on three sides were enhanced by natural scarping, while the fourth was given a double ditch. There is some confusion as to just how old the castle is, as references to it being burnt by Welsh raiders might in fact relate to Castell Stephan near Lampeter. The stronghold passed to William de Camville on his marriage to Albreda, daughter of Geoffrey Marmion, the first recorded lord of Llansteffan. It would remain in the de Camville family until the male line died out in 1338. It was captured and held briefly by the Lord Rhys in 1189, an episode that led de Camville into strengthening its defences and replacing wood with stone.

Right: LLANSTEFFAN CASTLE 1893 32798

CARREG CENNEN CASTLE

Standing on a 300ft limestone crag overlooking the Towy Valley, the present castle at Carreg Cennen dates from the late 13th century, though the site has historical links with the ancient commote (administrative area) of Is-Cennen, and sections of the south and west curtain walls might date from a castle held by Rhys Fychan in the 1240s. Late 13th-century work includes the gatehouse to the inner ward and the chapel tower; the barbican and outer ward are later. The castle was slighted by the Yorkists during the Wars of the Roses of the 15th century.

Below: CARREG CENNEN CASTLE 1936 87715A

PEMBROKE CASTLE

Pembroke Castle 1890 27957

Below: PEMBROKE CASTLE 1890   27955

Without doubt, Pembroke is one of the most impressive defended sites in Wales. The first castle was built by the Norman Roger de Montgomery and his son, possibly on the site of a Welsh fortification or fortified settlement. Pembroke was taken by Roger in 1093 during what can only be described as a scramble by Norman lords to help themselves to the lands of Rhys ap Tewdwr after his murder.

William Marshall's great cylindrical keep towers above the ruins. Built in the late 12th and the 13th centuries, the keep performed both residential and military roles. Its walls were the same thickness all the way up, which enhanced its defensive capabilities. All this may have inhibited the design of the two floors of residential apartments – though not the quality of their fittings. The top floor of the keep was primarily a fighting platform. It is, however, unlikely that the apartments were to be used except as a retreat of last resort, as the keep lacked a well and there were no garderobes (lavatories).

Construction of the outer wards was begun by William de Valence around 1260 and continued under Aymer de Valence. In shape it would form an irregular hexagon, with a tower at each of the angles. There was also a large gatehouse protected by a barbican, and the landward sides of the curtain wall were given a ditch defence. The future Henry VII is believed to have been born in one of the rooms of the gatehouse in January 1457.

MANORBIER CASTLE

The first castle at Manorbier was probably a motte and bailey erected by Odo de Barri. The castle underwent large-scale remodelling and extension over a 50-year period during the 13th century, much of the work being commissioned by John de Barri. The de Barris held Manorbier for 200 years until 1399, when it was declared forfeit to the Crown – this was because Sir David de Barri had supported Richard II. The earliest remains in stone are a hall and a small tower, both of which date from the 12th century. A famous resident from the 12th century was Gerald de Barri, born here in 1146, who is better known to us today as Giraldus Cambrensis, the author of the 'Itinerary of Wales', a valuable source of information for historians of the period.

Below: MANORBIER CASTLE 1893 32813

GIRALDUS CAMBRENSIS DESCRIBES MANORBIER, HIS FAMILY CASTLE

'The castle called Maenor Pyrr … is distant about three miles from Penroch. It is excellently well defended by turrets and bulwarks, and is situated on the summit of a hill extending on the western side towards the seaport, having on the northern and southern sides a fine fish-pond under its walls, as conspicuous for its grand appearance as for the depth of its waters, and a beautiful orchard on the same side, enclosed on one part by a vineyard and on the other by a wood, remarkable for the projection of its rocks and the height of its hazel trees. On the right hand of the promontory, between the castle and the church, near the site of a very large lake and mill, a rivulet of never-failing water flows through a valley, rendered sandy by the violence of the winds. Towards the west, the Severn sea, bending its course to Ireland, enters a hollow bay at some distance from the castle.'

Far Left: MANORBIER CASTLE, THE GATE AND THE DRAWBRIDGE 1890 27985

Left: MANORBIER CASTLE C1955 M24034

Below: HAVERFORDWEST, THE TOWN AND THE CASTLE 1890 27939

HAVERFORDWEST CASTLE

Haverfordwest was a sensible choice for a military settlement. The rocky outcrop on which the castle stands overlooks the tidal reaches of the Western Cleddau river, navigable to commercial and military traffic and also providing an obstacle to a land invasion from this direction. The first documentary evidence tells us that a castle was built here by a Fleming, Tancred, in 1110. In 1289 the town of Haverfordwest passed briefly into the ownership of Eleanor of Castile, the wife of Edward I. Although she died soon after in 1290, she spent large amounts of money on improving the castle. The castle was attacked by Owain Glyndwr in 1405, and by 1577 it was described as 'utterlie decayed', but there was a prison there then: 'a rounde tower, under which is a stronge prison house'. By the time of the Civil War the castle was deemed incapable of being seriously defended, and was slighted in 1648 under the orders of Oliver Cromwell to ensure that it would be of no further military use.

Above: Haverfordwest Castle, The Walls c1960 H41076

Below: ABERYSTWYTH CASTLE 1903 50810p

ABERYSTWYTH CASTLE

On 25 July 1277, Edmund, brother of Edward I, arrived in Aberystwyth to supervise the laying-out of the new castle and town. The site chosen for the castle was on the coast so that it could be supplied by sea, both for building materials (although it seems that some were shipped from Bristol to Carmarthen and thence by land) and also to give protection during times of attack. The castle stood on the boundary of the northern kingdom of Gwynedd and the Anglicised south, and it was a suitable site for a harbour. Aberystwyth was one of four castles that were started in 1277 – the others were Builth, Flint and Rhuddlan.

The castle took 12 years to complete, during which time it was attacked three times. The first attack occurred in 1282 when followers of Llywelyn the Last and others invited the constable of the castle to have a meal with them. They seized him, burnt the town and the castle, destroyed the town walls and killed the inhabitants, but they spared the garrison. After this, it appears that there was a change of plan under a new architect. The new building was to be completely concentric and a barbican was built to strengthen the entrance.

The town and castle were attacked for a second time in 1284, when Aberystwyth was besieged by the Welsh for about six months, but the occupants were relieved by supplies brought by sea. This rebellion was instigated by insensitive English administration and taxation, and began with the murder of Geoffrey Clement at Cardigan. He was custodian of Aberystwyth Castle, and during the siege of the castle his widow, Margery, took refuge in Aberystwyth. She appears on the list of burgesses in the town in 1307.

In 1287 the castle was attacked by Rhys ap Maredudd, but only part of the town wall was destroyed. The carpenters Robert and Nicholas were paid to 'put the castle on a war footing'. After the attack the Normans gathered a large army to fight Rhys. On 13 August 1287, 6,600 men commanded by 47 officers left Aberystwyth to join others in Cardigan. It is possible that this was to be the largest number of people to gather in Aberystwyth at one time until the coming of the railways.

The castle at Aberystwyth was built to the same concentric plan as most of the other castles built in Wales at the time – a castle within a castle with a massive gateway (shown in 30285); but unlike the other castles in Wales, it was thoroughly demolished by Parliamentarian forces in 1649 during the Civil War. In 1739 the Corporation announced that it would fine anyone caught removing stone from the castle. Towards the end of the century the owner laid out gravel paths around it and built a summerhouse on Castle Point for visitors.

In the 19th century the ragged remains of Aberystwyth's castle were transformed into public gardens by the local council and became a popular place for holidaymakers and trippers alike. In the photograph on the opposite page, the crowd gathers on a sunny afternoon to enjoy the antics of a pierrot troupe – they are the men on the far right in the white silk clown costumes and dunces' caps. The act would feature songs, jokes, mime and monologues.

Above: ABERYSTWYTH CASTLE 1892 30285

THE COST OF BUILDING ABERYSTWYTH CASTLE

The expenditure of almost every half penny spent on the castle was recorded and the original accounts survive, showing that it cost at least £4,300 to build. We know that William the plumber's assistant was paid 2d (just under 1p) per day and the master mason was paid 12d (5p) per day. Building work was not carried out during the winter months, so it is possible that hundreds of people were employed during part of the year, either at the castle or elsewhere, gathering, preparing and transporting materials.

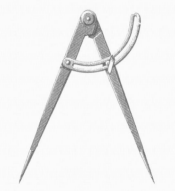

HARLECH CASTLE

When Harlech Castle was built, the sea lapped around the base of the craggy rock on which it stands. At sea level was the water gate, which allowed the fortress to be reinforced or supplied by ship. Any attacker capturing the water gate then faced a climb of 108 steps up the side of the crag to the next objective, an intermediate turret with a drawbridge. Attackers also had to run the gauntlet of artillery fire, possibly from trebuchets (see the box on siege warfare weapons on page 69), mounted on platforms near to the castle. These weapons, when handled by experienced crews, could be fired very accurately.

The twin-towered gatehouse (or Le Gemeltour Supra Portam as it was called in a survey of the castle undertaken in 1343) is seen above, flanked on the right by the Prison Tower (Le Prisontour), and on the left by the Garden Tower (Turris Ultra Gardinum). In the Prison Tower a trapdoor in the floor of the first floor was the only way in, or out, of a deep circular dungeon. A similar room also existed in the basement of the Garden Tower.

Left: HARLECH CASTLE 1889 21736

Above: HARLECH CASTLE 1889 21737

CRICCIETH CASTLE

Above: CRICCIETH CASTLE 1931 84766

Criccieth was a Welsh fortress, and was probably completed in the early 13th century by Llywelyn ap Iorwerth. It was captured by the English early in 1283, who immediately set about improving its defensive capability; Edward I committed a great deal of money to the project. Further work was carried out between 1287 and 1288, and the towers were heightened during the reign of Edward II. Criccieth became something of a hybrid: an Edwardian inner ward inside what was essentially a Welsh outer ward. In 1326 the garrison stood at ten men; their main defensive weapon was the crossbow, which fired a heavy, hard-hitting bolt that could penetrate armour at ranges up to 250 yards.

DOLWYDDELAN CASTLE

Five miles south-west of Betwys-y-Coed, Dolwyddelan Castle was founded about 1170 by Iorwerth Trwyndwn ('the Flatnosed'), and this was where his son Llywelyn was born. The castle was strategically sited so as to control the principal route between Nant Conwy and Meirionnydd by way of the Lledr Valley, and was Iorwerth's home for many years. It was captured by the English in January 1283 following the death of Llywelyn the Last. The surviving rectangular tower at Dolwyddelan is thought to have been built as late as 1270, possibly by Llywelyn ap Gruffydd as a two-storey structure. A third storey was added in the 15th century.

Left: DOLWYDDELAN CASTLE 1891 29541

Below: DOLWYDDELAN CASTLE 1891 29542

CAERNARFON CASTLE

Left: CAERNARFON CASTLE 1890 23112

Below Left: CAERNARFON CASTLE 1890 23116

Simultaneous construction of the castle and town wall at Caernarfon began in the summer of 1283. The Eagle Tower of the castle, which is considered by many to be a keep, was possibly built as a residence for Sir Otto de Grandison (1238-1328), the first justiciar of North Wales. He was a close and trusted friend of Edward I, and was also appointed constable of Caernarfon, a post he held for about four years. The fourth storey, battlements and turrets were added to the Eagle Tower in 1317. In 1620 the castle was in such a run-down state that only the Eagle Tower and the King's Tower were roofed. Photograph 23112 gives a good view of the banded masonry along the south front. Inspired by the Theodosian Wall at Constantinople, its use at Caernarfon was deliberate and designed to impress. All who saw it, especially the Welsh, had no doubt that they were looking upon the seat of a new royal government and a new imperial power. From left to right the towers are: the Eagle; the Queen's; the Chamberlain; and the Black. When the fortress was first built, the waters of the River Seiont lapped these southern walls.

In photograph 23116 we are looking towards the Eagle Tower, with the Queen's and Chamberlain Towers on the left. Between these latter towers once stood the 100ft-long Great Hall, which probably had a buttery and a pantry at its east end. There was direct access between the hall and the Chamberlain Tower, as well as steps leading down to a postern opening towards the River Seiont. The elevated entrance to the Queen's Gate was due to the fact that behind it lay the motte of the 11th-century castle built by Hugh de Lupus, Earl of Chester (he was nicknamed Lupus – the wolf – because of his ferocity). The Queen's Gate led directly into the royal inner ward and was approached by means of a ramp and drawbridge.

Below: CAERNARFON CASTLE 1890 23122

THE STRONG DEFENCE WORKS AT CAERNARFON

The high curtain wall at Caernarfon allowed the castle to be provided with three levels of defence: two levels of casemates, and the wall walk. Some of the embrasures were designed so as to allow bowmen to shoot in several directions from the same position. The King's Gate was the entrance to the lower or inner bailey; this side of the castle was defended by a moat, and there was once a drawbridge. The passageway of the King's Gate was protected by five doors, six portcullises, arrow loops, and murder holes in the vaulted ceiling.

Right: CONWY CASTLE 1898   42386

Below Right: CONWY CASTLE 1913   65753p

In March 1283 Edward I ordered Conwy Castle to be built and a burgh (or township) established. The choosing of the site was deliberate: here stood the royal hall of Llywelyn the Great (demolished in 1316) and the Cistercian Abbey of St Mary, where he lay buried. The castle was built on a steep ridge; the slope of the rock on the south side was such that it would have been impossible to mount an assault from that direction using battering rams or siege towers. Also, the curtain wall was too high for the scaling ladders of the day. Conwy Castle's drum-towers are almost identical in size and plan. All the towers were originally surmounted with round turrets, but only those on the inner ward towers have survived.

The king's apartments were on the first floor of the inner ward. Here was the Presence Chamber, where Councils would have been held. There was a smaller chamber for more private business, a chapel, and a lobby for guests to wait in before being received. The towers at the angle of the castle contained bedchambers for use by the king and queen. On the ground floor were apartments for the king's officials.

Because the curtain walls were so high, there were large areas of dead ground around the fortress that the defenders were unable to fire into with any accuracy. The north and west curtains faced the town and were considered vulnerable to assault should the town fall. The north curtain's defensive capability was enhanced by six embrasures at ground floor level. These enabled archers to fire upon any attackers attempting a direct assault upon the north curtain, and allowed them to target a section of the town wall. The west curtain was protected by its own barbican.

CONWY CASTLE

BEAUMARIS CASTLE

Beaumaris Castle was the last of Edward I's Welsh fortresses. Construction began in 1295 under the personal supervision of the king's engineer-architect, Master James of St George. Master James used Harlech Castle as the basis for the design, employing two large gatehouses instead of a keep. The walls were 15ft thick, and like the gatehouses they were flanked by six towers. Beaumaris was in fact never finished. War with Scotland, and Edward's desire to press his claims in France, meant that money was tight. The towers of the inner curtain were never completed to their intended height, and the great hall and other accommodation and domestic blocks in the inner ward were never begun.

The southern gateway of the outer bailey of Beaumaris Castle once guarded a small dock situated where the moat met a channel dug from the sea. Construction of the hexagonal outer bailey curtain wall along with its associated towers and gates began in about 1315, though the northern gateway is thought not to have been completed. The design included offsetting the gateways in such a way that any attackers would be forced to turn a corner before reaching the inner ward gatehouses, thus subjecting them to a murderous crossfire from nearby towers.

Above: BEAUMARIS CASTLE 1911 63307

Right: BEAUMARIS CASTLE, THE GATEWAY 1911 63302

FLINT CASTLE

Above: FLINT CASTLE c1955 F120040

The construction of Flint Castle began within days of the signing of the treaty of Rhuddlan in 1284; it was the first of the Edwardian fortresses built to impose a new order upon Wales. Work began in the summer of 1277 on both the castle and a new borough – the English had come to colonise as well as conquer. The borough was given a ditch and palisade, and the castle was built in stone from the start. Flint's castle was given a large but weak outer bailey, but the rectangular inner ward was supported with towers at the angles. The south-east tower, or donjon, had walls 23ft thick and was separated from the wall of the inner ward by its own moat and drawbridge. The curtain wall was once much higher, but was reduced when the castle was slighted during the Civil War. In 1399 Richard II was brought here after being intercepted by the Earl of Northumberland. Richard had returned from Ireland, landing at Milford Haven, and was on his way to Conwy to suppress a rebellion and meet up with his cousin, Henry Bolingbroke. Henry had other ideas: he wanted the throne for himself, and he had the support of a number of lords, including Northumberland. Richard was persuaded to ride to Flint with only a small escort of five esquires, and Northumberland was lying in wait for him. Richard was eventually taken to Pontefract Castle, where he died, either murdered or starved to death.

DENBIGH CASTLE

A DEADLY SPOT

DENBIGH CASTLE 1888   20851

The great triple-towered gatehouse of Denbigh Castle has an interesting design. The towers were arranged with two at the front and one at the rear, thus creating a small octagonal courtyard in the middle of them. This sounds very attractive, but any attackers reaching this point would be caught in a vicious crossfire from murder holes. The gatehouse was also defended by two portcullises and two doors.

Work on Denbigh Castle began in 1282 during the second of Edward I's Welsh wars. It was not a royal fortress, but was built by Henry de Lacy, Earl of Lincoln, although it was designed by the king's engineer-architect Master James of St George, and Edward I gave support. As with a number of fortresses raised at this time, Denbigh was deliberately built on a site that had meaning to the Welsh – in this instance a former residence of the princes of Gwynedd. During the revolt of 1294 the Welsh won a victory at Denbigh: it is unclear as to whether this refers to a pitched battle, or taking the castle, or taking the town, or a combination of these three. The English were soon back, and work continued on the castle, but it stopped again a few years later when Henry de Lacy, distraught at the death by drowning of his only son in the castle well, wanted nothing more to do with the place. Following de Lacy's death in 1311, the castle passed through a number of hands. Denbigh saw action during the Wars of the Roses in the 15th century, and changed hands on several occasions. In 1468 it finally fell to a Lancastrian force led by Jasper Tudor, Earl of Pembroke. Both the town and the castle were put to the torch; the damage to the former was such that when reconstruction started, much of the town was built outside the old walls.

Throughout the Civil War, both the town of Denbigh and its castle were held by the Royalists, and it was one of the last places to hold out against Parliament. The keys to the castle and the town were hurled at the feet of the Parliamentarian commander Major General Myddleton from the top of the Goblin Tower upon the surrender of the Royalist garrison. In 1647 Parliament ordered the withdrawal of its garrison, although slighting did not begin in earnest until 1660, when gunpowder was used. In the 19th century a walled-up chamber in the west gate was opened – it was found to be still full of gunpowder.

Above: DENBIGH CASTLE 1888   20853

Right: DENBIGH CASTLE c1960   D22106

CHIRK CASTLE

The present castle was begun in about 1283 by Roger Mortimer. There had been an earlier marcher stronghold at Chirk; it was either on this site or nearer to the village, where traces of a motte and bailey survive, but wherever it was it had long fallen into disrepair. When built, Chirk was an Edwardian square castle with a drum-tower at each angle, though by 1310 work was under way to extend it. The battlements were wide enough for two men to walk along side by side, and a principal feature was the castle's 160ft x 100ft quadrangle, the entrance to which can be seen in this photograph between two drum-towers. One of Chirk's more unusual claims to fame is that it was once besieged by its owner. During the Civil War it was garrisoned for the king, though its owner, Thomas Myddleton, was fighting for Parliament. Thomas laid siege to Chirk, but was unable to take it. At the end of the first phase of the war it was returned to him, but he changed sides when the second phase of the war broke out; he found himself besieged at Chirk by a Parliamentarian force commanded by General Lambert.

The splendid decorative iron gates shown on the right were made by the Davies brothers of Bersham (master craftsmen in wrought iron) between 1719 and 1721.

Above: CHIRK CASTLE c1869 5519

Right: CHIRK CASTLE, THE GATES c1955 C366118

Overlooking the Clyde to the north of the present town of Bothwell is its ruined castle, which is widely acknowledged to be one of the finest examples of secular architecture in Scotland, though it was never completed to its original design. It was built in about 1225 by John de Vaux, seneschal to Marie de Coucy, and its design is similar to the stronghold of Coucy in that it has a round donjon, as do the other Scottish castles of Kildrummy and Dirleton. Bothwell's donjon stood 82ft high, and it was 65ft in diameter; the walls were 15ft thick. Bothwell was taken by the English and retaken by the Scots a number of times; in 1298-99 it was under siege for fourteen months before the Scots managed to win it back, only to lose it again in 1301. It then remained in English hands until the time of the battle of Bannockburn, when it was surrendered to Edward Bruce. Following its slighting in 1337, Bothwell lay waste until 1362 when it was refortified. Excavations here have uncovered the largest assemblage of medieval pottery so far found on a single site; some of it is of local manufacture, some of it English.

BOTHWELL CASTLE

Above: BOTHWELL CASTLE 1897 39866

ROTHESAY CASTLE

Described in 1549 as 'the round castle of Buitte callit Rosay of the auld', the first stone castle was a circular shell keep 142ft in diameter with walls 30ft high and 9ft thick; four projecting drum towers were added in the 13th century. The design is unique. The original parapet survives, embedded in the stonework of the subsequent heightening of the curtain. The forework seen in 39845 is a high tower which extends into the moat and dates from a remodelling of the castle by James IV and James V. The tower served a dual purpose; it was both a strong gatehouse and royal apartments.

Right: ROTHESAY CASTLE 1897 39845

Below: ROTHESAY CASTLE 1897 39844

Below: DUNOON CASTLE 1897   39831

DUNOON CASTLE

This was once the seat of the FitzAlans, hereditary High Stewards of Scotland. Walter FitzAlan married Robert Bruce's daughter Marjory, and it was their son who was crowned Robert II, thus starting the Stewart (later Stuart) dynasty. Upon Robert's accession, the Campbells were appointed hereditary keepers of Dunoon. The knight's fee is 'one red rose when asked for'. All that survives of this fortress is the rock upon which it stood and a few traces of masonry.

Dumbarton Castle straddles the 240ft-high basalt rock that dominates the burgh. Protected on three sides by water, the rock was the ideal location for a fortification; for around 600 years it was the capital of the kingdom of Strathclyde. The oldest section remaining today is a 12th-century gateway; most of the buildings date from the 17th and 18th centuries. It was from here, in 1548, that six-year-old Mary, Queen of Scots left for France to marry the Dauphin when both were old enough. In return, France offered Scotland military assistance against England.

DUMBARTON CASTLE

Above: DUMBARTON CASTLE c1890 D62001

Below: CROOKSTON CASTLE, GLASGOW 1897 39808

CROOKSTON CASTLE

Crookston Castle was the first property to be acquired by the National Trust for Scotland. The estate was held in the 12th century by Sir Robert Croc of Neilston, and it is from him that the castle derives its name. In the 14th century the estate passed into the hands of Alan Stewart of Darnley. The tower was probably built in the early 15th century by Sir John Stewart, Constable of the Scots in the French service. In July 1565 Henry, Lord Darnley and Mary, Queen of Scots came to Crookston following their marriage; the castle at that time was owned by Darnley's father, the Earl of Lennox.

LOCHRANZA CASTLE

BRODICK CASTLE

This view was photographed near the northern tip of the island of Arran. A ruined 14th-century double-towered castle stands guard over Loch Ranza. It was here that Robert Bruce is said to have landed on his return from Ireland in 1306.

Above: ARRAN, THE CASTLE AND LOCH RANZA c1890   A93001p

Now owned by the National Trust for Scotland, Brodick Castle dates from the 14th century. It was from here in 1307 that Robert Bruce launched his campaign to liberate mainland Scotland from the English. The castle was enlarged when it was garrisoned by Cromwell's troops in the 17th century; the tower is a mid 19th-century addition.

Left: ARRAN, BRODICK CASTLE AND THE BAY 1890   A93002

DUART CASTLE

Above: DUART CASTLE, MULL c1890 M114001

Situated on a rocky site at the entrance to the Sound of Mull, the Maclean fortress of Duart dates from the 13th century with 16th- and 17th-century additions. The Macleans sided with Graham of Claverhouse ('Bonnie Dundee') when he raised the standard of James VII (James II of England) against William of Orange, who the Glorious Revolution had made William III; the clan held out against the forces of William until 1691. In 1715 they fought for the Stuart cause at Killicrankie and Sherrifmuir; their loyalty to 'the king over the water' was punished by the Campbells. In 1745 they fought for Prince Charles Edward Stuart, though it has been said that the core of this army was made up of clans hoping more to settle scores with Argyll and the Campbells than to worry too much about restoring the house of Stuart. Following the 1745 Jacobite uprising, Duart was garrisoned by government troops, but it was abandoned by the end of the 18th century and allowed to fall into ruin. It was eventually bought back by the Macleans, and has been restored.

Inveraray is set picturesquely on the shores of Loch Fyne, where it meets Loch Shira. Though now a substantial settlement, it was built on the site of a modest fishing village in the 18th century by the 3rd Duke of Argyll. He demolished the old village and constructed a grand castle, re-housing the local people in well-designed Georgian dwellings along the new main street.

The original castle at Inveraray was built about 1520. It was to Inveraray that MacIan of Glencoe was sent to swear allegiance to William III – his unavoidable delay in reaching Inveraray led to the massacre at Glencoe by William's forces in 1693. When the 3rd Duke of Argyll decided to build a new castle he engaged Roger Morrison as the architect and William Adam as the clerk of works. Work began in 1743 and ended in 1770. The new site was 80 yards or so from the old castle, which was demolished in 1773. Dr Johnson was entertained at Inveraray by the 5th Duke of Argyll.

Left: INVERARAY, THE CROSS, THE CASTLE AND DUNIQUAICH C1900 I15301

Below: INVERARAY CASTLE C1955 I15004

INVERARAY CASTLE

Above: DUNSTAFFNAGE CASTLE 1903 50886

DUNSTAFFNAGE CASTLE

Dunstaffnage belongs to the period when a determined effort was being made to extend royal power. The original fortress was to be used as a forward base against the Norse-controlled Hebrides. It was equipped with a high curtain wall 10ft thick, and round towers.

LINLITHGOW PALACE

Above: LINLITHGOW PALACE 1897 39154

THE FATE OF THE BODY OF JAMES IV

After the battle of Flodden in 1513, a half-naked corpse was later identified as being that of James IV of Scotland. The body was disembowelled, embalmed and sent to London. Katherine of Aragon was all for sending the corpse to Henry VIII who was campaigning in France, but instead it was sent to Sheen Abbey, where it eventually finished up being left in a lumber room. The remains were rediscovered by workmen some time after the Dissolution; it is said that they cut off the head and used it as a football. Before it was finally laid to rest in an unmarked grave, the king's disembodied head was kept as a curio by Lancelot Young, master glazier to Elizabeth I.

Situated half-way between Edinburgh and Stirling, Linlithgow became a favourite royal residence. David I built a manor at Linlithgow, and next to it a church dedicated to St Michael. During the wars with the English it was often under siege or counter-siege. In 1301 Edward I set about rebuilding and heavily fortifying the palace. It remained in English hands until the autumn of 1313, when it fell by deception: a hay-cart was driven under the portcullis to prevent it from being lowered. Mary, Queen of Scots was born here in 1542, and Prince Charles Edward Stuart stayed here in 1745.

The royal apartments were situated on the west side of the quadrangle. It was here that Queen Margaret kept vigil whilst the Scottish king, James IV, fought at the battle of Flodden in 1513. James was between a rock and a hard place. He was bound to France by the 'auld alliance', and also to England by an accord signed in 1502. Despite attempts to remain out of the coming war between England and France, he was eventually drawn into it. In August 1513 a Scottish force under Lord Home raided Northumberland, but was defeated when ambushed by Sir William Bulmer of Brancepeth. Flodden would be an even worse disaster for Scottish arms: their losses ran into thousands, and included 300 knights, nineteen barons, ten earls, a bishop, an archbishop, and James IV himself (see box opposite).

Linlithgow reached its final form during the reign of James V of Scotland, though the north wing was reconstructed in the neo-classical style between 1618 and 1633. The last Scottish national parliament was held here in 1646, and Oliver Cromwell lived at Linlithgow for several months following the battle of Dunbar. The palace was accidentally burnt down by General Hawley's troops in 1746. In this picture we can also see St Michael's Church, which was rebuilt in the 15th century.

Above Left: LINLITHGOW PALACE, QUEEN MARGARET'S BOWER 1897 39156

Right: LINLITHGOW PALACE 1897 39153

By the beginning of the 7th century the site occupied by Edinburgh Castle was a stronghold of the Gododdin, but in AD638 it fell to the Northumbrians, at that time the most powerful of the Anglo-Saxon kingdoms, whose territory stretched from the Forth to the Humber and to the south of the Mersey. The name of Edinburgh is thought to derive from 'Edwin's burgh' – Edwin was King of Northumbria in the 7th century. Edinburgh Castle was to become one of the most advanced castles of its time; many of the natural features of the site were incorporated into the plan to make the best possible use of them. However, when the English King, Edward I, besieged the castle in 1296, he deployed giant catapults to batter the garrison into submission, and succeeded in obtaining their surrender after three days and nights of rock-dodging.

Edinburgh Castle became the principal residence of Malcolm III (1058-93) and his wife Queen Margaret. The earliest surviving structure, Queen Margaret's Chapel, dates partly from c1100. When Robert Bruce captured Edinburgh Castle from the English in 1313 he gave orders that this chapel should be left unharmed, although all else was destroyed to prevent the English making military use of the castle in the future. Edinburgh Castle looks impregnable. However, an inherent weakness in the defences was the lack of water. The fortress is perched high on a cliff of carboniferous basalt, and the main well is 89ft deep. Though supplies under normal conditions were adequate, excessive demand during periods of dry weather would lead to its drying up. During the slighting of the castle in 1313, Robert Bruce ordered the well to be filled in, and its location was lost until 1381.

EDINBURGH CASTLE

Opposite: EDINBURGH CASTLE, FROM
THE GRASSMARKET 1897 39121t

Right: EDINBURGH CASTLE 1897 39121AP

In 1314 Edinburgh Castle was in English hands, held by Peres Lebaud, Edward II's Sheriff of Edinburgh. It was recaptured for the Scots by Thomas Randolph, Earl of Moray. An assault force led by William Francis made their way along an old track up the north precipice, scaled the walls, opened the gates and let in the main Scottish force. In 1341 Edinburgh Castle was again in English hands, this time occupied by the troops of Edward III, under the command of Guy, Count of Namur. The Scots used a cunning plan to win back the castle: William of Douglas disguised himself and his men as merchants bringing supplies to the garrison. They dropped their loads so that the gates could not be closed; then they held on fighting until joined by the main force, whereupon they took back the castle. Of the English garrison of 49 men-at-arms, 60 archers and six watchmen, most were butchered, and their bodies were flung over the walls onto the crags where they were left to rot.

The castle that we see today is, with a few additions, the one built by the Earl of Morton following the siege of 1572. Morton succeeded Lennox as Regent, and took the fortress in the name of the infant James VI from the supporters of Mary, Queen of Scots. It was Morton who added the great Half-Moon Battery to the castle's defences, seen in photograph 39121t – the parapet was added in the 1690s. Behind the battery are the palace and the Great Hall. On this side of the castle stand most of the buildings constructed before 1625 which have survived above ground level in a recognisable form.

When the Duke of Gordon held the castle for James VII (James II of England) during the Long Siege of 1689 by the forces of William of Orange, there would have been few, if any, buildings between the fortress and the port of Leith. Gordon surrendered the castle on 13 June 1689 owing to sickness and acute shortages of food and water. Between 1988 and 1991, excavations unearthed the remains of some of the garrison from this siege. None of the skeletons showed signs of wounds, but all appeared to have died from disease.

Although Bonnie Prince Charlie managed to occupy Edinburgh in 1745, he failed to capture its fortress, which was held by forces loyal to the Hanoverian King George II.

The Esplanade, or parade ground, was laid out in its present form in the 1820s. Of the castle buildings, on the left of the photograph above is the palace (reconstructed in 1617), the Half-Moon Battery and Forewall Battery. Each weekday at 1pm a cannon is fired from the Half-Moon Battery as a time check, a tradition which began in 1861. The small tower on the right with the angled roof is the Portcullis Gate, the upper part of which was added in 1886-87. In this photograph a battalion of the Black Watch parade on the castle esplanade. Raised by General Wade in 1725, the Black Watch was formerly constituted as a regiment of the line in 1739, and its strength was increased from four to ten companies.

THE SCOTTISH NATIONAL WAR MEMORIAL

In the Palace Yard of Edinburgh Castle is the Scottish National War Memorial, unveiled in 1927. This commemorates the 100,000 Scots who died in the First World War. In bronze and stained glass, the memorial depicts every type of war service imaginable, including the contribution of the transport mules, the carrier pigeons, and even the mice and canaries used to detect gas in the mines and trenches.

James III commissioned the construction of Mons Meg, a mighty weapon for its time; it made a great hole in James's defence budget, just as it did in anything it was fired at. Deploying Meg was a logistical nightmare: when James IV ordered it to be dragged to the siege of Norham Castle in 1497, it took over 220 men and 90 horses to get it there. In 1680 the cannon burst when it fired a royal salute to Charles II.

Below: EDINBURGH CASTLE, MONS MEG C1950   E24001p

THE KNIGHT AND HIS ESQUIRES

When a knight was merely going for a ride or on a journey, he usually bestrode a sober kind of hack that was called a palfrey, but when he was going to take the field, one of his esquires led at his right hand (whence the name of destrier given to this sort of steed) a charger or high horse, which the knight only mounted at the last moment. Hence the expression, 'to ride the high horse', which has become proverbial.

As soon as the knight had decided to mount his charger, his esquires proceeded to arm him, that is to say, they firmly fastened together all the different pieces of his armour on his body with straps attached to metal buckles for the purpose; and it may be well conceived that no slight care was required to properly adjust such a cumbrous and complicated steel or iron casing; an esquire's neglect, indeed, frequently caused his master's death.

When a single combat took place, the esquires, drawn up behind their lord, remained for a few moments inactive spectators of the struggle, but as soon as it had once fairly begun their share in the affray commenced. Watching the slightest movement, the smallest signals of their master, they stood ready to assist him in an indirect but efficacious manner if he attained any advantage, without actually becoming aggressors themselves, in order to assure his victory; if the knight were hurled from his steed, they helped him to remount, they brought him a fresh horse, they warded off the blows that were aimed at him; if he were wounded and placed hors de combat, they did their utmost, at the risk of their own life, to carry him off before he was slain outright. Again, it was to his esquires that a successful knight confided the care of the prisoners he had taken on the battlefield. In fine, the esquires, short of actually fighting themselves, a thing forbidden by the code of chivalry, were expected to display the greatest zeal, the greatest skill, and the greatest courage, and consequently had it very materially in their power to contribute to their master's success.

From 'Military and Religious Life in the Middle Ages' (1874), Paul Lacroix

ROSLIN CASTLE

Founded by Sir William Sinclair, Roslin dates from the early 14th century. Sir William's grandson built a keep which was enlarged by the 3rd Earl of Orkney in the 1440s. During the English invasion of 1544 the castle was effectively destroyed, but was rebuilt in 1580. Further additions were made during the 17th century.

Right: ROSLIN CASTLE 1897 39166

Roslin's chapel, a few hundred yards from the castle, is famous for its 'Prentice Pillar' of entwined ribbands. The story is that the chief stonemason went to Italy to study a similar pillar. While he was away, his apprentice worked out how to construct the pillar after having a dream, and built it. When the stonemason returned, he was so jealous of his apprentice's work that he struck the boy dead. On the chapel walls are sculptured heads of the mason, the boy and his weeping mother.

Top Left: ROSLIN CASTLE 1897 39165

Top Right: ROSLIN, THE CHAPEL, THE INTERIOR 1897 39164A

Above: ROSLIN, THE CHAPEL 1897 39164

TANTALLON CASTLE

Tantallon was a stronghold of the Douglases, a powerful family who were wardens of the Border Marches, lords of Galloway, and by the end of the 15th century masters of much of Lothian, Stirlingshire and Clydesdale. James V resented the Douglases, and besieged Tantallon in 1528. 'Red Douglas' held out for three months before surrendering. He was lucky to be allowed to go into exile, his estates forfeited to the Crown, since another victim of James's vendetta, Lady Glamis, was burned at the stake for alleged witchcraft.

Even in its ruined state, Tantallon still looks formidable. The great curtain wall with its central gatehouse, flanked at either end by a massive round tower, dates from the last quarter of the 14th century. The gatehouse incorporated the castellan's quarters and represents a shift away from the keep or donjon to the keep-gatehouse.

Left: TANTALLON CASTLE, NORTH BERWICK 1897 39186

Below: TANTALLON CASTLE, NORTH BERWICK 1897 39187

LOCH LEVEN CASTLE

Though there was a castle at Loch Leven that withstood a siege in 1335, the five-storey tower house seen here dates from the late 14th to the early 15th century. The entrance to the tower is on the second floor and reached only by a ladder. Loch Leven has a small irregular courtyard, known as a barmkin, which is enclosed by a curtain wall. Mary, Queen of Scots was imprisoned here by the lords of the Congregation in 1567 and compelled to abdicate in favour of her son James VI. The following year she escaped and joined her army, which was commanded by the 5th Earl of Argyll.

Above: LOCH LEVEN CASTLE c1890 L2355001

Opposite: SCONE PALACE FROM THE NORTH-WEST 1899 43914

In 1581 Scone was given to the Earl of Gowrie. Following the forfeiture of his lands in 1600, it passed into the ownership of Sir David Murray of Gospetrie. He and his descendants extended the house built by the Earl of Gowrie, but at the turn of the century the decision was taken to build a new palace. This was designed by William Atkinson. Work began in 1803 and finished in 1808. As with Inverary Castle, the redevelopment meant the removal of the whole village, which in this case had grown up round the Augustinian monastery which was destroyed in 1599. A new village of Scone was laid out a mile and half away, allowing the palace to be set in extensive parkland. All that now remains of the old village are the cross and the graveyard.

THE STONE OF DESTINY

Scone is of course associated with the Stone of Destiny. This is thought to have been a portable altar that once belonged to an early missionary from Iona or Ireland. The stone, on which the Scottish kings were crowned, was brought to Scone in AD843, but was stolen by Edward I in 1296 and taken to England, where it was kept in Westminster Abbey under the Coronation Chair. It was supposed to be returned to Scotland under the terms of the Treaty of Northampton (1328), but it was not actually given back until St Andrew's Day 1996.

LONDON, WESTMINSTER ABBEY,
THE CORONATION CHAIR c1890 L130265

SCONE PALACE

Situated three miles south-west of Crieff, Drummond Castle was originally built by John, 1st Lord Drummond, in 1491. It has endured its share of troubles: it was besieged and bombarded by Cromwell, destroyed in 1689 and subsequently rebuilt, garrisoned by Hanoverian troops in 1715, and finally partially dismantled by the Jacobite Duchess of Perth to deny it to the English and their allies.

Drummond Castle was owned by the Drummond family, earls of Perth; Sir Malcolm Drummond fought beside Robert the Bruce at Bannockburn in 1314 and was granted lands in Strathearn. Sir John Drummond built the castle there in 1491. His daughter Margaret was James IV's mistress, but the Scottish nobles wanted James IV to marry Margaret Tudor, sister of Henry VII of England, and arranged to have Margaret Drummond murdered. The 6th Earl of Perth was one of Bonnie Prince Charlie's commanders at Culloden in 1746 – after the defeat of the Jacobites, the Drummonds lost their castle and lands. Today the castle is owned by the Earls of Ancaster, descendants of the Drummonds. The wonderful parterre gardens, among the finest formal gardens in Europe, were originally laid out in the early 17th century by the 2nd Earl, Privy Councillor to James VI and Charles I. The unique sundial has about 50 faces, so as to tell the time all over Europe.

Above: DRUMMOND CASTLE, CRIEFF 1899　44359

Below: DRUMMOND CASTLE, CRIEFF, THE GARDENS 1904　52938p

DRUMMOND CASTLE

Situated to the south-east of the town on the left bank of the River Teith at its junction with the Ardoch, Doune Castle derives its name from the Gaelic word 'dun', meaning 'a fortified place'. It differs from the earlier great castles such as Kildrummy and Bothwell in that the living apartments are incorporated into the gatehouse. In older castles the practice was to position them to the rear of the courtyard. Doune was conceived as a courtyard castle, but was never finished. It was built by Robert Stewart, 1st Duke of Albany, Guardian of Scotland, on behalf of the captive James I. Robert died in 1420 and his lands and titles passed to his son Murdoch. In 1424 King James returned to Scotland after spending eighteen years as the 'guest' of the English court. He was also angry that, in his eyes, Robert Stewart had done precious little to secure his freedom during that time. With the 1st Duke already in his grave, the king's revenge fell upon Murdoch and other members of the Stewart family. Arrested, tried for treason and condemned, Murdoch was executed. Doune was then used as a royal residence until 1528 when it was returned to a descendant of Albany. The principal feature of the castle is the four-storey keep-gatehouse which rises 95ft high. It is flanked by a five-storey round tower, and the small ruined structure corbelled out from it on the left (first floor) of 44646 is in fact a privy and not a doorway.

In 44648 we see the western end of the lord's hall following its restoration. The work included relaying the floor with red, black and buff tiles based on the recovered fragments of the originals, and the fitting of oak wall panelling, the screen and the music gallery. It was from here that the portcullis was operated. When Doune was first built there were no interconnecting doorways between the keep-gatehouse and the retainers' hall.

Above Right: Doune Castle from the North-East 1899 44646

Right: Doune Castle, The Lord's Hall 1899 44648

DOUNE CASTLE

STIRLING CASTLE

Above: STIRLING CASTLE FROM KING'S KNOT 1899 44693

Stirling was a royal castle during the reign of Alexander I, and he is thought to have died there in 1124. One of Scotland's greatest royal fortresses, Stirling Castle was to change hands a number of times during the Wars of Independence between Scotland and England. The castle was taken by William Wallace in 1297, but was abandoned by the Scots following Wallace's defeat at Falkirk. Once again the English took possession, strengthening their fortifications, but in 1299 Edward I failed to relieve the garrison besieged by John Comyn, Lord of Badenoch and Bishop Lamberton of St Andrews; the Constable, John Sampson, was eventually forced to surrender, and the castle was again in Scottish hands. Following another siege, the castle was surrendered by the Scots to Edward I in August 1305. The survivors of the garrison, commanded by Sir William Oliphant, were brought before Edward and made to kneel in supplication.

Both James II and James V of Scotland were born at Stirling, and Mary, Queen of Scots and James VI (James I of England) also lived here for a number of years. When the forework was remodelled for James IV, it partially followed the line of earlier defences. The main gatehouse was supported by flanking half-drum towers and the curtain wall had a rectangular tower at each end, though they were of different sizes owing to the geography of the site. During the 1530s James V spent a large amount of money refurbishing Stirling as well as building a new palace. The design is thought to be French-influenced; several of the king's masons were of French origin, and two were Dutch.

A few miles south of Stirling is Bannockburn; in 1314 this was the site of the decisive battle where Robert Bruce's Scots defeated Edward II's ten times stronger English army. This victory resulted in the surrender of Stirling Castle to the Scots and recognition by the Pope of Robert Bruce's kingship, eventually culminating in Scottish independence.

The Napoleonic Wars led to a severe shortage of barrack accommodation in Scotland. Additional space was found by remodelling the great hall of the castle at Stirling to create twelve barrack rooms. The work included inserting additional floors, cross walls, staircases, windows and doorways.

'THE HAMMER OF THE NORTH'

Edward I is often referred to as 'The Hammer of the North' because of his campaigns into Scotland, but originally he planned to take control of Scotland through diplomatic means, with the betrothal of his son Edward (later Edward II) to Alexander III's grand-daughter Margaret, known as 'the Maid of Norway' because she was the daughter of Eric II of Norway. In 1284 the nobles of Scotland recognised her as heiress to the Scottish throne, but Edward's plan came to nothing when the Maid was drowned whilst travelling to Scotland. Scotland was then left with no clear heir to the crown, and many years of warfare ensued between claimants supported by Edward and other rival Scottish nobles.

Left: STIRLING, THE BRUCE STATUE 1899 44681

Below Left: STIRLING CASTLE, OLD PARLIAMENT HOUSE 1899 44697

Below Right: STIRLING CASTLE 1899 44696

CAWDOR CASTLE

INVERLOCHY CASTLE

The 13th-century Inverlochy Castle, home of the Comyn family, is built in the form of a square, with round towers at the corners. Set on the banks of the River Lochy, it is one of Scotland's earliest stone castles, and it was here in February 1645, after a forced march across difficult terrain in appalling weather, that the Marquess of Montrose with 1,500 troops defeated a 5,000-strong force of Campbells and Lowlanders. The clan power of Argyll is said to have been destroyed for a generation at Inverlochy.

Left: INVERLOCHY CASTLE c1890 I30001

A few miles to the south of Nairn stands Cawdor Castle, one of Scotland's finest medieval buildings. It is famous for its associations with Macbeth and the murder of Duncan in Shakespeare's 'Scottish play'. The central tower of the castle dates from 1454, when the thane was given permission to erect Cawdor 'with walls and ditches and equip the summit with turrets and means of defence, with warlike provisions and strengths ... provided that it would always be open and ready for the King's use and his successors'. The castle was extensively altered during the 16th and 17th centuries, and again in the 19th.

Left: CAWDOR CASTLE 1890 C212001

Below: CAWDOR CASTLE c1890 C212301

Below: BRAEMAR CASTLE C1960 B266001

BRAEMAR CASTLE

Braemar Castle is a five-storey L-plan tower-house, which was built by the Earl of Mar in 1628. Although Braemar was burnt down by Graham of Claverhouse in 1689, it was rebuilt. The curtain wall was added when the castle was used as a garrison for government troops. It was here in August 1714 that a so-called hunt was assembled by John Erskine, 6th Earl of Mar. It was in fact the start of the Jacobite rebellion against the house of Hanover and the Union, and the Stuart standard was raised.

BALMORAL CASTLE

The first documented evidence for a castle at Balmoral dates from 1484, when it was known as Bouchmorale and held by Alexander Gordon. By the end of the 18th century it was owned by the Earl of Fife, and in 1830 it was leased by Sir Robert Gordon, who hired the architect William Smith to remodel the old castle. Queen Victoria and Prince Albert made their first visit to Balmoral in 1842. Victoria fell in love with the place because she loved the walks and rides the estate offered; Albert loved it because it reminded him so much of his native Thuringia. Following Sir Robert's death in 1847, Victoria and Albert were offered Balmoral; however, the royal couple were not sufficiently wealthy to be able to buy the estate and carry out the required alterations. Help came from the eccentric barrister John Camden Neild, who bequeathed Victoria £500,000 'for her sole use and benefit', and it is thanks to Neild's generosity that Balmoral exists in the form it does today. Prince Albert hired the architect William Smith, and together they worked on creating one of the finest examples of Scottish baronial architecture. Built of Invergelder granite quarried on the Balmoral estate, the castle comprises two ranges joined together by an 80ft tower, and is able to accommodate up to 120 people.

Above: BALMORAL CASTLE FROM THE SOUTH-WEST
c1890 B268002

Left: BALMORAL CASTLE c1890
B268001

It was Sir William Keith, Marischal of Scotland, who built a tower house at Dunnottar in the late 14th century, and is said to have been excommunicated for his trouble by the Bishop of St Andrews for building on sacred ground – the site had been occupied by the parish church of Dunthoyr since the 1270s. A Bull from Pope Benedict XIII removed the excommunication when Sir William built another church. The site, an isolated 150ft-high rock, is ideal for a fortress. The tower house is of the L-plan type (rectangular with a small wing at right-angles). The tower is separated from the rest of the fortress by a deep ditch, wall and gatehouse. Dunnottar was equipped for artillery, though the military efficiency of the frontal battery is open to question, as the guns could not be brought to bear on the entrance. The corner tower, however, is equipped with wide-mouthed ports allowing the defenders to cover any attempt to climb the slopes. Following Charles II's defeat at the battle of Worcester, Dunnottar was the only fortress over which the royal standard of the house of Stuart remained flying. In May 1652 Dunnottar was besieged by General Lambert for eight months in an attempt to seize the royal regalia of Scotland and the king's private papers. The regalia were smuggled out under the skirts of the minister of Kinneff's wife, and the papers by Anne Lindsay.

DUNNOTTAR CASTLE

Above: DUNNOTTAR CASTLE c1900 D80401

THE WEST COUNTRY

Berkeley Castle 23

Compton Castle, Torquay 19

Corfe Castle 21, 22

Dunster Castle 20

Polruan 18

Restormel Castle 16, 17

St Catherine's Castle, Fowey 17

St Mawes Castle 13

St Michael's Mount Castle 14-15

Sandsfoot Castle, Weymouth 22

Tintagel Castle 10-11, 12

LONDON AND THE SOUTH COUNTRY

Arundel Castle 35-36

Bodiam Castle 38

Carisbrooke Castle 31, 32, 33

Dover Castle 42

Guildford Castle 30

Hastings Castle 37

Hever Castle 40-41

Leeds Castle 39

Portchester Castle 34

Rochester Castle 43, 44

Saltwood Castle 41

Tower of London 24-25

Windsor Castle 26-29

Windsor Castle, St George's Chapel 27

THE MIDLANDS AND EAST ANGLIA

Castle Rising 56

Colchester Castle 54

Kenilworth Castle 47, 48

Kirby Muxloe Castle 49

Newark-on-Trent Castle 50

Norwich Castle 55

Nottingham Castle 50, 51, 52-53

Tattershall Castle 57

Warwick Castle 45, 46, 47

THE NORTH

Bamburgh Castle 85

Barnard Castle 81

Bolsover Castle 58

Brougham Castle, Penrith 80

Bolton Castle, Castle Bolton 76, 77

Castle Rushen, Castletown 64, 65

Clitheroe Castle 59

Conisbrough Castle 66-67, 68

Durham Castle 82, 83

Holy Island 86-87

Knaresborough Castle 70

Lancaster Castle 60-61, 62

Middleham Castle 74, 75

Newcastle upon Tyne Castle 84

Peel Castle 63

Pontefract Castle 68, 69

Richmond Castle 71, 72-73, 74

Scarborough Castle 78-79

WALES

Aberystwyth Castle 114-115

Beaumaris Castle 123

Caernarfon Castle 120, 121

Caerphilly Castle 100

Cardiff Castle 94-95, 96-97

Carreg Cennen Castle 108

Chepstow Castle 88-89, 90

Chirk Castle 126

Conwy Castle 122

Criccieth Castle 118

Crickhowell Castle 93

Denbigh Castle 125

Dolwyddelan Castle 119

Flint Castle 124

Harlech Castle 116-117

Haverfordwest Castle 112-113

Llansteffan Castle 106-107

Manorbier Castle 111-112

Newport Castle 98

Ogmore Castle, Bridgend 101

Oxwich Castle 103

Oystermouth Castle 102

Pembroke Castle 109, 110

Pennard Castle 105

Raglan Castle 90-91

St Donats Castle 98, 99

Swansea Castle 102

SCOTLAND

Arran, Brodick Castle 132

Arran, Lochranza Castle 132

Balmoral Castle 152-153

Bothwell Castle 127

Braemar Castle 151

Cawdor Castle 150

Crookston Castle, Glasgow 131

Doune Castle 147

Drummond Castle, Crieff 146

Duart Castle, Mull 133

Dumbarton Castle 130

Dunnottar Castle 154

Dunoon Castle 129

Dunstaffnage Castle 135

Edinburgh Castle 138, 139, 140

Inveraray Castle 134

Inverlochy Castle 150

Linlithgow Palace 136, 137

Loch Leven Castle 144

Roslin Castle 141, 142

Roslin Chapel 142

Rothesay Castle 128

Scone Palace 145

Stirling Castle 148, 149

Stone of Destiny 144

Tantallon Castle, North Berwick 143

The Francis Frith Collection Titles

www.francisfrith.com

The Francis Frith Collection publishes over 100 new titles each year. A selection of those currently available is listed below. For our latest catalogue please contact The Francis Frith Collection.

Town Books 96 pages, approximately 75 photos. **County and Themed Books** 128 pages, approximately 135 photos (unless specified). Pocket Albums are miniature editions of Frith local history books 128 pages, approximately 95 photos.

Accrington Old and New
Alderley Edge and Wilmslow
Amersham, Chesham and Rickmansworth
Andover
Around Abergavenny
Around Alton
Aylesbury
Barnstaple
Bedford
Bedfordshire
Berkshire Living Memories
Berkshire Pocket Album
Blackpool Pocket Album
Bognor Regis
Bournemouth
Bradford
Bridgend
Bridport
Brighton and Hove
Bristol
Buckinghamshire
Calne Living Memories
Camberley Pocket Album
Canterbury Cathedral
Cardiff Old and New
Chatham and the Medway Towns
Chelmsford
Chepstow Then and Now
Cheshire
Cheshire Living Memories
Chester
Chesterfield
Chigwell
Christchurch

Churches of East Cornwall
Clevedon
Clitheroe
Corby Living Memories
Cornish Coast
Cornwall Living Memories
Cotswold Living Memories
Cotswold Pocket Album
Coulsdon, Chipstead and Woodmanstern
County Durham
Cromer, Sheringham and Holt
Dartmoor Pocket Album
Derby
Derbyshire
Derbyshire Living Memories
Devon
Devon Churches
Dorchester
Dorset Coast Pocket Album
Dorset Living Memories
Dorset Villages
Down the Dart
Down the Severn
Down the Thames
Dunmow, Thaxted and Finchingfield
Durham
East Anglia Pocket Album
East Devon
East Grinstead
Edinburgh
Ely and The Fens
Essex Pocket Album
Essex Second Selection
Essex: The London Boroughs

Exeter
Exmoor
Falmouth
Farnborough, Fleet and Aldershot
Folkestone
Frome
Furness and Cartmel Peninsulas
Glamorgan
Glasgow
Glastonbury
Gloucester
Gloucestershire
Greater Manchester
Guildford
Hailsham
Hampshire
Harrogate
Hastings and Bexhill
Haywards Heath Living Memories
Heads of the Valleys
Heart of Lancashire Pocket Album
Helston
Herefordshire
Horsham
Humberside Pocket Album
Huntingdon, St Neots and St Ives
Hythe, Romney Marsh and Ashford
Ilfracombe
Ipswich Pocket Album
Isle of Wight
Isle of Wight Living Memories
King's Lynn
Kingston upon Thames
Lake District Pocket Album

Available from your local bookshop or from the publisher

The Francis Frith Collection Titles (continued)

Lancashire Living Memories
Lancashire Villages
Lancaster, Morecambe and Heysham Pocket Album
Leeds Pocket Album
Leicester
Leicestershire
Lincolnshire Living Memoires
Lincolnshire Pocket Album
Liverpool and Merseyside
London Pocket Album
Ludlow
Maidenhead
Maidstone
Malmesbury
Manchester Pocket Album
Marlborough
Matlock
Merseyside Living Memories
Nantwich and Crewe
New Forest
Newbury Living Memories
Newquay to St Ives
North Devon Living Memories
North London
North Wales
North Yorkshire
Northamptonshire
Northumberland
Northwich
Nottingham
Nottinghamshire Pocket Album
Oakham
Odiham Then and Now
Oxford Pocket Album
Oxfordshire
Padstow
Pembrokeshire
Penzance
Petersfield Then and Now

Plymouth
Poole and Sandbanks
Preston Pocket Album
Ramsgate Old and New
Reading Pocket Album
Redditch Living Memories
Redhill to Reigate
Richmond
Ringwood
Rochdale
Romford Pocket Album
Salisbury Pocket Album
Scotland
Scottish Castles
Sevenoaks and Tonbridge
Sheffield and South Yorkshire Pocket Album
Shropshire
Somerset
South Devon Coast
South Devon Living Memories
South East London
Southampton Pocket Album
Southend Pocket Album
Southport
Southwold to Aldeburgh
Stourbridge Living Memories
Stratford upon Avon
Stroud
Suffolk
Suffolk Pocket Album
Surrey Living Memories
Sussex
Sutton
Swanage and Purbeck
Swansea Pocket Album
Swindon Living Memories
Taunton
Teignmouth
Tenby and Saundersfoot
Tiverton

Torbay
Truro
Uppingham
Villages of Kent
Villages of Surrey
Villages of Sussex Pocket Album
Wakefield and the Five Towns Living Memories
Warrington
Warwick
Warwickshire Pocket Album
Wellingborough Living Memories
Wells
Welsh Castles
West Midlands Pocket Album
West Wiltshire Towns
West Yorkshire
Weston-super-Mare
Weymouth
Widnes and Runcorn
Wiltshire Churches
Wiltshire Living Memories
Wiltshire Pocket Album
Wimborne
Winchester Pocket Album
Windermere
Windsor
Wirral
Wokingham and Bracknell
Woodbridge
Worcester
Worcestershire
Worcestershire Living Memories
Wyre Forest
York Pocket Album
Yorkshire
Yorkshire Coastal Memories
Yorkshire Dales
Yorkshire Revisited

See Frith books on the internet at www.francisfrith.com

FRITH PRODUCTS & SERVICES

Francis Frith would doubtless be pleased to know that the pioneering publishing venture he started in 1860 still continues today. Over 140 years later, The Francis Frith Collection continues in the same innovative tradition and is now one of the foremost publishers of vintage photographs in the world. Some of the current activities include:

INTERIOR DECORATION
Today Frith's photographs can be seen framed and as giant wall murals in thousands of pubs, restaurants, hotels, banks, retail stores and other public buildings throughout the country. In every case they enhance the unique local atmosphere of the places they depict and provide reminders of gentler days in an increasingly busy and frenetic world.

PRODUCT PROMOTIONS
Frith products are used by many major companies to promote the sales of their own products or to reinforce their own history and heritage. Frith promotions have been used by Hovis bread, Courage beers, Scott's Porage Oats, Colman's mustard, Cadbury's foods, Mellow Birds coffee, Dunhill pipe tobacco, Guinness, and Bulmer's Cider.

GENEALOGY AND FAMILY HISTORY
As the interest in family history and roots grows world-wide, more and more people are turning to Frith's photographs of Great Britain for images of the towns, villages and streets where their ancestors lived; and, of course, photographs of the churches and chapels where their ancestors were christened, married and buried are an essential part of every genealogy tree and family album.

FRITH PRODUCTS
All Frith photographs are available framed or just as mounted prints and posters (size 23 x 16 inches). These may be ordered from the address below. From time to time other products - address books, calendars, table mats, etc - are available.

THE INTERNET
Already 100,000 Frith photographs can be viewed and purchased on the internet through the Frith website and a myriad of partner sites.

For more detailed information on Frith companies and products, look at this site:

www.francisfrith.com

See the complete list of Frith Books at: www.francisfrith.com
This web site is regularly updated with the latest list of publications from The Francis Frith Collection. If you wish to buy books relating to another part of the country that your local bookshop does not stock, you may purchase on-line.

For further information, trade, or author enquiries please contact us at the address below:
The Francis Frith Collection, Frith's Barn, Teffont, Salisbury, Wiltshire, England SP3 5QP.
Tel: +44 (0)1722 716 376 Fax: +44 (0)1722 716 881 Email: sales@francisfrith.co.uk

See Frith products on the internet at www.francisfrith.com

FREE PRINT OF YOUR CHOICE

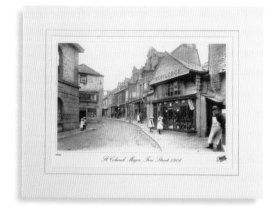

Mounted Print
Overall size 14 x 11 inches (355 x 280mm)

CHOOSE A PHOTOGRAPH FROM THIS BOOK

Choose any Frith photograph in this book.

Simply complete the voucher opposite and return it with your remittance for £3.50
(to cover postage and handling) and we will print the photograph of your choice in SEPIA
(size 11 x 8 inches) and supply it in a cream mount with a burgundy rule line
(overall size 14 x 11 inches).

Offer valid for delivery to UK addresses only.

PLUS: **Order additional Mounted Prints at HALF PRICE - £8.50 each** (normally £17.00)
If you would like to order more Frith prints from this book, possibly as gifts for friends and
family, you can buy them at half price (with no additional postage and handling costs).

PLUS: **Have your Mounted Prints framed**
For an extra £14.95 per print you can have your mounted print(s) framed in an elegant
polished wood and gilt moulding, overall size 16 x 13 inches
(no additional postage and handling required).

IMPORTANT!

These special prices are only available if you use this form to order.

You must use the ORIGINAL VOUCHER on this page (no copies permitted).

We can only despatch to one UK address.

This offer cannot be combined with any other offer.

Send completed voucher form to:
The Francis Frith Collection, Frith's Barn, Teffont, Salisbury, Wiltshire SP3 5QP

Voucher for *FREE* and Reduced Price Frith Prints

Please do not photocopy this voucher. Only the original is valid, so please fill it in, cut it out and return it to us with your order.

Picture ref no	Page no	Qty	Mounted @ £8.50	Framed + £17.00	Total Cost £
		1	Free of charge*	£	£
			£8.50	£	£
			£8.50	£	£
			£8.50	£	£
			£8.50	£	£
			£8.50	£	£
			* Post & handling		£3.50
			Total Order Cost		£

Please allow 28 days for delivery. Offer available to one UK address only

Title of this book. . . . .

I enclose a cheque/postal order for £ . . . .
made payable to 'The Francis Frith Collection'

OR please debit my Mastercard / Visa / Maestro card,
details below

Card Number

Issue No (Maestro only)   Valid from (Maestro)

Expires   Signature

Name Mr/Mrs/Ms . . . .

Address . . . .

. . . .

. . . .

. . . . Postcode . . . .

Daytime Tel No . . . .

Email . . . .

ISBN 0-7537-1443-4

Valid to 31/12/09

Can you help us with information about any of the Frith photographs in this book?

We are gradually compiling an historical record for each of the photographs in the Frith archive. It is always fascinating to find out the names of the people shown in the pictures, as well as insights into the shops, buildings and other features depicted.

If you recognize anyone in the photographs in this book, or if you have information not already included in the author's caption, visit the Frith website at www.francisfrith.com and add your memories.

Our production team

Frith books are produced by a small dedicated team at offices in the converted Grade II listed 18th-century barn at Teffont near Salisbury, illustrated above. Most have worked with The Francis Frith Collection for many years. All have in common one quality: they have a passion for The Francis Frith Collection. The team is constantly expanding, but currently includes:

Paul Baron, Jason Buck, John Buck, Jenny Coles, Heather Crisp, David Davies, Natalie Davis, Louis du Mont, Isobel Hall, Chris Hardwick, Neil Harvey, Julian Hight, Peter Horne, James Kinnear, Karen Kinnear, Tina Leary, Stuart Login, Sue Molloy, Sarah Roberts, Kate Rotondetto, Eliza Sackett, Terence Sackett, Sandra Sampson, Adrian Sanders, Sandra Sanger, Julia Skinner, Lewis Taylor, Will Tunnicliffe, David Turner and Ricky Williams.